DRYLAND

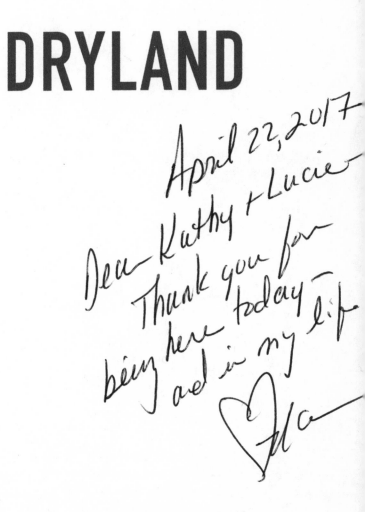

April 22, 2017

Dear Kathy + Lucie

Thank you for
being here today—
and in my life

♡

DRYLAND

ONE
WOMAN'S
SWIM
TO
SOBRIETY

a memoir

NANCY STEARNS BERCAW

GRAND
HARBOR
PRESS

Published by Grand Harbor Press, Grand Haven, MI

www.brilliancepublishing.com

Amazon, the Amazon logo, and Grand Harbor Press are trademarks of Amazon.com, Inc., or its affiliates.

ISBN-13: 9781503942950
ISBN-10: 1503942953

Cover design by Janet Perr

Printed in the United States of America

For David

إنه نفس المطر الذي كنت تعشقه.. أغرقك

It's the same rain you loved that drowned you.

—*Arabic Proverb*

PART I:

BEFORE

THE PERSIAN GULF

March 27, 2015

I have one pill left—a single twenty-milligram dose of my antidepressant. Unless I find a way to get a refill tomorrow, I'm in trouble. Besides getting weepy, I'll go' into withdrawal. The contents of my head will feel like they're moving independently from the forces of gravity. The vertigo will be so extreme that I'll have to hold on to walls, chairs, and stairwells. The nausea will become so unbearable that I'll vomit wherever I am.

One must be weaned from most antidepressants; going cold turkey isn't an option. I know because I tried once. I first started taking them when I was pregnant with my son, David, because I was having panic attacks. I was scared that the life growing inside me would get so big that my lungs wouldn't be able to expand and contract properly. Irrational, I know. But behind the veil of lung capacity I was hiding larger fears about being a mother. The antidepressants helped me breathe again.

Why did I wait until the last possible day to deal with my need for a refill? I've been watching the days count down yet did nothing to intervene in the fate coming at me like a bullet. The answer has as much to do with where I am as who I am.

I live in Abu Dhabi, in the United Arab Emirates, in the Middle East, and I have no idea how to get this particular substance. I came here with eight months' worth and the assumption that I'd figure out how to get more when the time came. But which doctor do I see? Is he or she even allowed to dispense a serotonin reuptake inhibitor? What questions will be asked of me? How do I explain my depression when I don't even understand it myself?

Why would someone like me, who fears untimely death more than anything, move to the Middle East in the midst of a terrorist insurgence? My husband had a job offer to be the head of a film school here, but he didn't have to accept it and we didn't have to come. Allan had retired from a long career in filmmaking a few years back. We had a perfectly nice life on the shores of Lake Champlain in Vermont, where I worked at the University of Vermont.

Although Abu Dhabi is a quiet, peace-loving oasis on the Persian Gulf, a number of hostile nations lie just across the sea. The shores of Iraq are a mere 460 nautical miles away. Airspace is closed over the surrounding countries of Syria, Iraq, and Yemen. Afghanistan, Pakistan, and Libya round out the region's complicated hot spots. Living in Abu Dhabi is akin to being a minnow in a fishbowl next to a tank of piranhas. You're safe unless the glass breaks.

I've come to rely on wine to silence my fears about being here— or anywhere, for that matter. Alcohol helps me forget a lot of things, including my family history of Alzheimer's disease. When my grandfather came down with the memory-stealing malady in 1965, my father, who was in medical school at the time, made the decision to specialize in neurology. He hoped to find a way of preventing Alzheimer's from taking root in his own skull as well as the heads of his patients.

His strategy failed. Dr. Beauregard Lee Bercaw died on April 2, 2012, at the age of seventy-three—the exact same age at which his father had succumbed to the exact same disease. Based on my uncanny physical resemblance to my paternal lineage, I figure I'm probably the next Bercaw up to bat. My father actually planted the idea in my head before he got sick, telling me that both of us were destined for Alzheimer's disease. "No ifs, ands, or buts," he said. "We're getting it."

Subconsciously, I probably came to Abu Dhabi to have more tangible things to fear. Psychiatrists call this a counterphobic attitude—seeking out fearful situations. But I thrive on overcoming challenges, the lingering results of twenty years as a competitive swimmer. Perhaps I also came here, on the verge of fifty, to win out over something in me.

If there is a way to get what I want, I'll find it. And what I want these days is alcohol, lots of it, to fill some sort of bottomless swimming pool inside of me. Buoyed by booze, I drift away from what scares me and I feel powerful again. But getting a dose of liquid courage is a whole other challenge.

Consuming, buying, or possessing alcohol is illegal for Muslims in Abu Dhabi. Non-Muslim expats can obtain booze in hotel bars or private clubs, or at a handful of liquor stores. I prefer the latter, despite the associated complexities.

Every time, I have to explain to a cabdriver how to get to Spinneys, the liquor store. The conversations are troublesome, considering our language, gender, and cultural differences. Cabdrivers in Abu Dhabi are almost always male immigrant laborers from India, Pakistan, Bangladesh, Nepal, and Uganda. They work long hours and reside in labor camps outside the city. My request to stop at Spinneys is as perplexing as it is rare.

On one particular occasion, a driver couldn't resist asking about my purchases.

"Are you drinking every day?" he asked in pretty good English, staring at me in his rearview mirror. He sipped from an imaginary bottle to be sure I understood. "Does your husband know? Is he home?"

The way he looked at me was jarring, chilling. Was he envious that my religion let me drink? Did he want to take advantage of me if my husband wasn't home and I was intoxicated? Was he just curious about the ways of the West?

"No," I lied, adding another: "We are having a party tonight to celebrate eighteen years of marriage."

He nodded but continued to glare at me through the mirror. I turned away to watch the cars pass and to catch glimpses of the Gulf between high-rises, but every time I looked back, his eyes were still on me. Was he watching the road at all?

"Where are you from?" I asked. Determined to never visit wherever it was.

"Pakistan."

"Which city?"

"Islamabad."

When we arrived at Spinneys, I paid the fare and sent him on his way. He was probably harmless, despite his curiosity about my husband's whereabouts and my boozing, but his question about "every day" unnerved me. I preferred silence when it came to my relationship with alcohol.

The Spinneys windows are blackened with plastic bags and duct tape to keep the faithful from being tempted by the store's products. Inside, other expats fill their carts with booze. More often than not, I shop alongside Indian construction workers who are buying the cheapest liquor possible with what remains of their very modest income after having sent the bulk of it back to their families on the subcontinent. My heart hurts for their difficult circumstances, so I grab a handful of minibar-sized vodka bottles at the checkout counter to assuage the added pain in my emotional shopping cart of sadness.

Shoppers at Spinneys have to present a liquor license to make their purchases. This form of identification, which proves non-Muslim status, is a bureaucratic nightmare to obtain. The foremost requirement, for those from countries where Islam is a major religion, is a certificate from your house of worship confirming your denomination. At five feet ten inches, blonde and blue eyed, I'm so blatantly obviously an American Christian that the proprietor doesn't ask for my ID card, which I never bothered to obtain anyway.

I have given myself free rein to drink with a vengeance while I am in Abu Dhabi, even though I take antidepressants. I need a full arsenal to combat the invisible terrorists in my head—which feel like a far greater threat to my existence than the ISIS rebels in nearby countries.

I always leave Spinneys with a clanking black bag full of wine and vodka. I normally try to muffle the telltale noise with my purse or jacket, by moving very slowly, but when the temperature is more than 120 degrees, I just walk quickly—and noisily—back to the air-conditioned cab where ten-year-old David is waiting for me in the backseat. I routinely entrust him to a stranger in a strange land so I can buy the stuff that makes me forget who and where I am.

Sometimes David goes home from school with a friend, and sometimes Allan picks him up and takes him to see the film students in action. On those occasions, I shop more leisurely in Spinneys to evaluate the specials. Sometimes wine is buy-five-get-one-free, which is my favorite deal because it seems like the free bottle is also a free pass to imbibe more.

When we arrive at our home in the Mangrove Place apartments—a modest brown-cement building dwarfed by the surrounding tall glass ones, with nary a mangrove in sight—David and I usually go down to the pool. Swimming is the only real antidote to the 120-degree heat. I slather sunscreen all over my very pale son and myself. The sun here has the strength to turn us bright red in less than an hour.

David does his homework in a lounge chair. I take note of the slender young European women in bikinis, working on their tans. They smoke cigarettes and read paperback books. I watch the pool boy, from somewhere in Africa, use a ruler to draw straight lines in the log where each of us has to register our name and unit number. There are signs posted on every wall telling us not to pee in the pool and not to drink alcohol on the deck. I adhere to both rules even though I suspect others don't.

Whenever David and I have the pool to ourselves, I do a few fast laps to show my son how it's done. For those fleeting minutes, I'm back to being one of the best swimmers in the United States. A seventeen-time All American; an Olympic Trials qualifier in the 50-meter freestyle; a national champion who strutted her slender body around swim decks like she owned them.

Afterward, I stand in the shallow end and stare through the glass wall at the waterways leading to the Persian Gulf. *Look how far I've come,* I lament. The endorphins I once got from Olympic-sized swimming pools in Florida now come only from alcohol in the Arabian Desert.

Since moving here, I've suffered from one singular worry. Not whether Spinneys will run out of booze or whether the region will erupt in war. Instead, I've been preoccupied with the day I run out of antidepressants. My version of D-Day. And it arrives tomorrow.

Even if a doctor can give me a refill, what will he or she say about my general health?

I know my blood pressure is elevated from drinking a martini, a bottle of wine, *and* a nightcap every single night. I have chronic heartburn and stomach cramps from the amount of alcohol I consume. I look nothing like the great swimmer I once was. I'm thick around the middle. My once long, lean legs look more like tree stumps these days. My eyes are red, but not from chlorine. The lines around my eyes are from chronic exhaustion and age, not swim goggles. Between my natural freckles and the sun damage acquired by swimming in the Florida sun throughout my youth, I look sort of like an aging giraffe.

Swimming a handful of fast laps in the very short pool at Mangrove Place defeats me. I'm not who I was, or who I thought I'd be. I'm a pudgy giraffe on the Persian Gulf. Every inch of me is out of sorts and out of place.

When David and I go back upstairs to our apartment on the seventh floor, he retreats to his bedroom to play video games. He's pretty nonchalant about living in Abu Dhabi, but then again he's ten and in his own little world.

I've mastered the art of hiding the full extent of my drinking from David and Allan. My son sees most grown-ups enjoying "happy hour" around dinnertime, so I give myself free rein between five and seven p.m.

I think David sees my habit as the norm, not the exception, thanks to all the years I've been doing it and all the places we've lived where other expats do likewise. But I crossed the line somewhere along the way. Where was it, exactly? Kenya? Korea? Singapore? Hard to tell. Seems like it all just snuck up on me.

Allan has tiptoed around my alcohol use for years—either cautioning me not to go overboard or jumping off with me. He's the kind of person who can have one glass with dinner and call it a night. He's also the kind of person who can party into the night, maintaining a happy buzz by pacing himself. Once I start, though, I can't stop. I drink the way I used to swim: all or nothing. Truthfully, "nothing" was never an option. It was always "all."

At precisely five p.m. on March 27, 2015, I fill a glass with ice-cold vodka from the freezer and swallow down my last antidepressant with the first gulp. I'll deal with the reality of being out of medicine when the sun rises in the morning and the local mosques start calling the faithful to prayer. In the meantime, I'll sit on the couch in our tiny living room and drown myself from the inside out.

THE GULF OF MEXICO

July 4, 1976

In the summer of 1976, my hometown of Largo, Florida, was awash in red, white, and blue in honor of America's bicentennial. So too was my whole swim team, our Speedos covered with stars and vertical stripes.

I was eleven, skinny and sunburned. But in the water, I was more than the sum of my fledgling parts. I was larger than my life—faster than anyone else my age and many far older. My American-flag swimsuit made me feel even more powerful, as if the whole country was depending upon me to rise and shine.

I was certain that 1976 was the year I'd make my mark on the world, just as my country had two hundred years earlier, and just as American freestyler Shirley Babashoff was poised to do in the Montreal Olympics in the weeks to come. I was certain that I'd have the chance to represent my country in the Olympic Games one day.

I already had a dozen gold medals from Florida's Junior Olympics to my name. And I'd accumulated a total of ninety-nine trophies from all the other competitions I'd been winning since age six. They were lined up on the shelves in my bedroom, and I counted them, like sheep, before falling asleep. I was certain that having one more would make me happy, a feeling that always seemed just out of reach.

My dad promised to install as many shelves as were needed: *Just keep winning. Never stop. This is what you were born to do.* It seemed like he wouldn't be happy until our house was a wall-to-wall trophy case.

◆ ◆ ◆

He was the one who taught me to swim. I was three years old, and we were living in Huntsville, Alabama, while he did a residency in neurology. One hot summer day, he took me to a nearby river for my first lesson. My mother had asked if we could join the local country club to swim, but my father refused on principle.

"Free water runs rampant," he said. "I'm not paying to swim in some."

Both of my parents had been raised on farms in Virginia, managing with little during the Depression. And both of their families had done well after the hard times, accumulating moderate wealth from investments. But my father was particularly hell-bent on teaching me the value of a dollar as well as the fine art of being a "river rat." If the two lessons could be learned in tandem, he told my mom, then little Nan would be well ahead of the game. I was little Nan, named for his mother, Nancy Scott Bercaw.

At the river, my dad waded in waist deep—which would have been shoulder deep for most other people, since my dad was taller than anyone I'd ever met. I waited on a rock at water's edge for instructions from my giant coach.

"Okay, gal," he said. "Jump off the rock and get to me as fast as possible."

I had no idea how to comply, so I sat down to think about what he was asking me to do.

"Stand up! Jump! Swim!" he yelled. "Don't hem and haw like some first-class wimp!"

I threw myself into the river and aimed my flailing limbs toward him. When I arrived on the island of my father, he erupted with enthusiasm.

"Fantastic, gal, you did it! You can do anything you put your mind to! Do it again, and faster!"

He hugged me and pushed me back toward the rock. I swam in the reverse direction with more confidence. I crawled up and jumped toward my dad again. I understood that it was a game I could win. Swimming offered more than a way to get toward my dad, it also delivered him to me. I was all that mattered when we were in the water.

"Imagine that a cottonmouth moccasin snake is chasing you," he said before my second jump. "If it bites your feet, you'll be dead in less than an hour! Even I can't save you! Swim as if your life depends upon it!"

So I did. Over and over again. In his loudest voice, my father counted out the seconds it took me to swim to him—1, 2, 3, 4, 5, 6, 7, 8, 9, and 10. After my fastest swim of the day, he lifted me onto his shoulders. I was his connection to the sky, he was my connection to the river bottom.

◆ ◆ ◆

We relocated to Florida when I was five. My father joined a private practice in Largo to start his career in brain medicine. When he told the other doctors about my swimming skills, they mentioned a private yacht club at the northernmost end of Clearwater Beach, where a certain swim coach was notorious for churning out the fastest sprinters in the entire state. Dad decided on the spot that I should be on the team. My mom was surprised that he was willing to join, considering the exorbitant fees.

"I'm investing in her," Dad said. "Her natural speed. Maybe she'll get a scholarship to swim in college."

My mom thought it was good for each of us to have an outlet. A place where Dad could play tennis and she could play bridge while I trained with the other kids.

"Your father works too much," she told me, with a hand on her pregnant belly. My little brother was due any minute.

For the next ten years, I swam two hours a day, six days a week, in the club's pool. My brother, Lee, joined the team when he turned five, but he preferred the club's milkshakes to swim practice.

I loved winning more than swimming, especially the delicious surge of adrenaline that came over me as I neared the end of a race. The sudden and magical high gave me the strength to overtake rivals as if I were a cheetah and they were antelopes, just like I'd seen on *Wild Kingdom*'s Sunday-evening television broadcasts. I came to think of myself as a big-game hunter and everyone in the pool as my prey. Instead of carcasses, though, I brought home trophies.

On July 4, 1976, our club hosted an Independence Day invitational swim meet. When I walked onto the pool deck that morning, a long row of trophies on the officials' table caught my eye. I found the one that said *High Point Award 12 & Under Girls*. To earn it, I'd have to win more races, and thereby more points, than any other girl in my age group. Essentially, I had to win at winning. Adrenaline coursed through my bloodstream at the very thought of that trophy being number 100 in my collection.

The meet of seven teams and hundreds of swimmers lasted all day. I swam four races, taking first place in each one—even backstroke, my weakest event. I anchored two relays, catching and surpassing the competition for those wins too. As I ran toward my father with the gleaming high-point trophy in my arms, I heard my coach say, "Nancy swam faster today than she's actually capable of doing."

To which my father replied, "She's capable of anything."

THE PERSIAN GULF

March 27, 2015

David is asleep in bed. Allan is working late at his school. I'm propped up in bed with my computer and my fifth glass of wine. I might drink another glass before Allan gets home. I don't necessarily hide how much I consume, but I do try to push my limits before he arrives. Sufficiently buzzed, yet still steady on my feet, I usually greet him at the door and offer to share a nightcap with him like I'm doing him a favor. He usually declines, so I pour one for myself. He never knows how many I've already had—or does he?

I try to balance my wineglass on my lumpy stomach. When it nearly falls onto my keyboard, which is on top of my thighs, I catch it with my still-lightning-fast reflexes and put it on the side table.

Almost all of my physical actions, on land or sea—or in bed—are executed for the greatest efficiency and the least resistance. I grind the coffee in the morning at the same time I'm pouring water into the coffeemaker. Whenever possible, I perform tasks simultaneously rather than sequentially. On nights like this, I fill my wineglass to the very top to reduce the frequency of trips to the fridge. Being efficient increases the amount of time I have for drifting away.

Tonight, I think about the day our family arrived in Abu Dhabi eight months earlier—trying hard *not* to think about how much alcohol I've consumed since then. If I lined up those bottles on a shelf, like the trophies of my youth, they'd outnumber one hundred by a landslide. But I dispose of the evidence, long before it has a chance to add up, in stealthy trips to the trash bin. If no one sees or hears me, then maybe my actions don't exist, like a tree falling in a forest, or however that saying goes.

I wonder what Mangrove Place's maintenance workers—all migrant laborers from Sri Lanka—think about the sheer volume of empty bottles in the refuse. They aren't all mine, thank God. Many of the American and European residents here drink up a storm too. The ugly proof of our excess is whisked away by those who live in labor camps outside the city.

Why do expats in Abu Dhabi drink so much? I'm not the only one. But I have a long history of drinking overseas. I'm a champ at this lifestyle. I see newcomers to the international experience as amateurs. There's a hierarchy, at least in my mind, of those who live overseas. And I'm at the top.

There are many rungs of expat existence in Abu Dhabi. But the Emirates occupy a whole other ladder entirely. Foreigners and locals aren't at odds, the way I felt in Seoul twenty-six years earlier. Emiratis do their thing and we do ours, which happens to include drinking like fish. Instead of gathering for prayer, Westerners get together to complain about the heat and find relief from it.

Our mecca is the former British Club, now simply referred to as "the Club" with hundreds of members hailing from America, Europe, and Australia. Membership is expensive but comes with access to a number of restaurants, two pools, and one beachfront. You can drink anywhere you want at the Club—in the water, on the diving board, in a bikini. Inside the gates, we're exempt from the strict social limitations of Islam and removed from our own histories. People like me forget that limits, lines, and borders even exist because we're so far out of bounds.

Sometimes I overhear a certain group of old men, who are always playing a game of mah-jongg at a table by the pool, lamenting the deteriorating situations in Syria and Iraq.

"If ISIS comes here, where will I go?" the elder statesman has said often. I can't tell where he's from originally, but it doesn't seem to matter. The question is where to next. The three other men at his table shrug. There's never an answer.

On my first day at the Club, a very slender and beautiful Eastern European woman, wearing a bikini with gold chains around her waist, sought me (the obvious newcomer) out to share her insight for living in Abu Dhabi.

"You will get fat and lazy here," she warned in a thick Slavic accent, long brown hair flying in the wind. "Do your housework yourself, don't hire anyone. Don't eat all this bread they serve. Don't trust these people. Don't trust anyone. I hate this place. I hate it. But the money. We make so much. My husband has no job in America, so we come here. Three years now. We're stuck. I hate it. So will you. I hate everything. Even the fleas on the stupid cats at this club."

She wandered off to talk to an older man who'd arrived on the pool deck. I heard someone else say that he was an exiled poet from Iraq and all the ladies loved him.

Whom exactly was the Eastern European woman telling me not to trust? Which people? The only person I wanted to steer clear of, thus far, was her. I'd already made pals with Jesus, a server from the Philippines, who delivered big plastic cups of cold white wine to my chair. I tipped Jesus very well for bringing me salvation.

"You are a big white Filipina!" he'd said when I told him of my birth at Clark Air Base.

With drink in hand, I listen to conversations between other people with drinks in their hands. They all mourn the damage ISIS is doing to the region, to historical sites and great populations of people. Yet I hear nothing about the damage we're doing to ourselves by drinking so much.

◆ ◆ ◆

Despite my own chronic overindulgence, I manage to get up every morning at six o'clock to give David breakfast and get him on the bus for the American International School. Carrying out the routine is proof that I haven't gone off the deep end.

Afterward, I shower and dress before taking a cab to the Arab university where I work as a writer and editor. I dress as conservatively as possible, in long tunics layered with loose pants. Because of the outside temperatures, my menopausal symptoms, and my hangovers, I'm usually drenched in sweat upon arrival. I'm not required to cover my long hair, although perhaps I should. When it blows around in the desert wind, I look like a blonde Medusa with stringy split ends reminiscent of fork-tongued snakes.

I am the lone American in my office. My eight colleagues in the Communications Department represent six nations: the UAE, Syria, Palestine, Bahrain, India, and Canada. All Emiratis on campus wear their national attire: men in white *kandora* robes, women in black *abaya* dress. They look so elegant, regal. Their clothing always perfectly pressed. Their myrrh-and-frankincense perfumes perfectly anointed. My female colleagues' makeup never smears, runs, or feathers. They arrive looking perfect; they leave looking perfect. I arrived disheveled and depart even more so.

I purchased an expensive perfume at a falconry exhibit—scents are available at every single venue in town, even the convenience store— but my fragrance goes bad the second it hits my alcohol-infused skin. I inevitably wind up smelling more like a bathroom sprayed with Febreze than a frankincense-infused Bedouin princess.

Behind their conservative traditions and cultural attire, my coworkers are modern young people who speak their minds and converse freely with the opposite sex. In Abu Dhabi women can make eye contact with men, a social norm strictly forbidden less than two hundred miles away in Saudi Arabia.

I've seen our lead event planner, a gregarious woman named Habiba, berate male employees and contractors for not doing as they were told. I've seen our head designer, Fareed, who is a bachelor at age thirty-nine, subtly flirt with the single women from Accounting. He drives a matte-black Mustang and takes lunchtime strolls through the glitzy local malls. I've often wondered what he's shopping for exactly. If I were single and twenty years younger, I'd succumb to handsome Fareed's desire for anything. I keep these thoughts to myself even as I steal glimpses of his angular face and deep, dark eyes.

My colleagues tease me about being an American and some of our perplexing pastimes.

"You going to brunch on Saturday?" our photographer, Imad, asked me one Thursday afternoon—the last day of the workweek. "Hump day" in the Middle East is Tuesday, not Wednesday. I always put a small one-humped-camel statue on my desk to mark the occasion and in anticipation of the hump-day happy hours to come.

On Tuesdays, as a family, we often go to dinner at Trader Vic's, located inside one of the main hotels. Inside, Allan and I sip fancy Tahitian-style cocktails from ridiculous drink vessels. David enjoys looking at the fish tanks, having a Shirley Temple, and eating food he recognizes. The band plays salsa music, and we all forget about being in the Middle East for a little while.

Imad's question about brunch made me laugh.

"What's wrong with that?" I asked, well aware of the problem with champagne for Muslims. Indeed, champagne was a problem for me because I loved it so much. I saw it as the main reason to eat an expensive buffet breakfast at a four-star hotel.

"It's a white-people thing!"

"Aren't you white?" I asked. Imad's skin was just a shade darker than my own.

He stood up tall and proud from his desk and announced, "We check the box marked *other*." I howled with laughter, as did the rest of the staff.

When I first arrived, I had no idea how much I would come to adore my colleagues and Abu Dhabi. All I knew, in late August 2014, was that the city was burning hot, temperatures pushing 120 degrees. And all I wanted to do was swim in the lukewarm sea at the Club, where cold beer and wine were never far from reach.

On our first day in Abu Dhabi, a longtime American resident of the city gave us a tour in her air-conditioned sports car. While explaining the confusing street signs and navigating the chaotic traffic, she casually remarked how the island city of Abu Dhabi was shaped like a uterus.

"What?" I made her repeat the statement.

"Abu Dhabi is shaped like a uterus."

I pulled out my iPhone to check the accuracy of her analogy.

"Yes, it is!" I said. "Exactly!"

From the backseat, David asked what a uterus was.

"It's where babies grow in their mothers," I answered, wondering why I hadn't yet told him about the birds and bees. I wasn't even sure when the right time to do so was, because I'd pretty much lost track of time altogether in recent years—a strange turn of events for someone like me, whose entire young life had been measured against the clock.

◆ ◆ ◆

I can feel myself drifting off to sleep in the bed I share with Allan, who still isn't home. No doubt his students are filming a scene and taking pains to get it right. Allan won't leave the school until everyone else has gone home. I send him a text of a heart blowing a kiss, and an icon of an old-fashioned cinema camera. He texts me back a camel and a swimmer.

Allan doesn't understand why I don't swim for exercise, even though I've told him the reason at least a dozen times.

"Water is for winning, not for swimming. I hate swimming. There's no reason to do it unless I'm gonna win an award or break a record. I'm not like all those people who say swimming laps brings them peace and quiet. It's not quiet or peaceful for me. Being a sprinter is an act of violence. Who's going to give me a trophy for surviving it again?"

"Okay," he says, resigned and confounded. Allan is a musician, as well as a filmmaker, and once played the lead role in the musical *Hair* on Broadway. He sings joyfully throughout the day, wherever he goes. I have told him repeatedly that the minute he starts hating music is the minute I'll start swimming again. In other words: *never*.

Swallowing the last drops of my last glass of wine for the evening, I've almost forgotten the mission to be accomplished come morning— getting a refill of my embarrassing medication in my embarrassing state of disrepair. I embrace the numbness enveloping me and float away. Even the sound of my wineglass shattering on the floor means nothing.

THE OHIO RIVER

December 15, 1979

By age fourteen, I'd earned the nickname "Nance Romance" because boys were very interested in swimming's effect on my body. I was muscular and lean, suntanned and bubbly. The guys seemed more interested in possessing me than actually speaking to me, as if I were a living and breathing version of the trophies I coveted.

My mother warned me to steer clear of their roving hands, but I liked it when the boys grabbed me in a rough embrace, leaving red marks on my back. I also liked to slip from their clutches before they could feel me up. In my swimsuit, I was a formidable presence. Once dressed, I was an awkward teenager like everyone else my age.

My swimming prowess had a remarkable effect on a lot of people. My parents' friends at the club constantly expressed their amazement. I'd heard a few of them had placed bets on whether I'd go to the Olympics one day. Everyone seemed so proud of me, but most especially my father.

Usually preoccupied by his patients' life-threatening illnesses, Dad rarely paid much attention to our family during the week. But on swim-meet Saturdays, he stood on deck with my mother and my brother, Lee, to cheer me on. He took lots of pictures with his fancy Canon camera, mostly of me holding blue ribbons. Lee swam a few races too, but he wasn't up to speed, according to our father.

Meanwhile, Dad screamed, "That's my gal!" whenever I finished first, which was all the time. He kept track, in his head, of how my results compared to local and state records. He'd give a status update after each race, with one of his long arms wrapped around my shoulders.

"You're only half a second off the Junior Olympics cut!" he remarked once, deciding the performance was worth a two-armed bear hug.

My dad prized excellence above everything—in medicine, in the swimming pool, and elsewhere. He took me to hear the inspirational speakers who came through town on the lecture circuit. Jacques Cousteau's overseas tales and underwater discoveries, in particular, entranced me.

For weeks after the Frenchman's lecture, I'd sing the refrain from John Denver's song "Calypso" as a greeting when my father got home from the office and hospital rounds.

My dad and I would walk, holding hands, into our living room, which was flanked on each side by sliding glass doors. We could see our driveway, lined with palm trees, out front. And we had a view of our boat dock and the murky canal leading to the Gulf of Mexico in the back. But the fishbowl design also meant that people on the street or on the water could look right into our home. I took comfort in the fact that there wasn't much to see other than silent people walking around on terrazzo floors.

If Mom or Lee wanted to connect with Dad before his attention turned to medical journals, they had only a brief window to do so after I'd shared the news from swim practice. Mom would give him a quick update on her work as a schoolteacher. Lee would ask about watching television later. The answer to Lee's question was always no.

"Go read a book," Dr. Bercaw would say before taking up with his own research and demanding quiet. My brother and I privately referred to him as "Dr. Bercaw" when he was in this distant mode. We spoke of him as "Beau" when he was remote yet still reachable.

Dinnertime was a solemn family affair unless a big meet was on the horizon, in which case Dr. Dad wanted to discuss how neuroscience could be applied to my strategy. Mom and Lee would have to watch us volley ideas back and forth in a game of verbal ping-pong across the dining table. My brother saw these conversations as an opportunity to hide his vegetables under his napkin. My mother would pour herself more Chablis.

"Gal, do you think your reaction off the block could be even faster?"

"If I can hear the starter move his finger before he actually pulls the trigger, I could jump sooner."

"That would shave about .25 seconds off."

"I'd make the Junior Olympic cut."

"What about your finish? Can it be stronger? Reach with everything you've got."

"I need to make my kick more powerful. Rise up, like a speedboat on overdrive."

"What if you held your breath for the whole race and didn't waste time turning your head?"

"I might be faster, or I'll go into oxygen debt."

"Try it. See what happens."

"It's risky, Dad."

"Fortune favors the bold, gal. That's what Virgil said."

One thing my father and I both knew for certain was that the higher the stakes, the faster I was likely to perform. The phenomenon fascinated him as much as any neurological disease. He could find no medical explanation for my unique relationship to distance, speed, and time. I, however, was pretty sure it had something to do with my relationship to him.

When my coach asked if we'd be willing to go to Cincinnati for a national meet in December of 1979, not only did my father say yes, but he also took four days off work to come along. Lee was left behind with a babysitter and a pile of frozen television dinners. I think he rejoiced in having the house to himself and someone to pay attention to his Lego projects instead of hearing about his sister's swimming all the time.

The fifty-meter pool in Cincinnati was the first Olympic-sized one I'd ever seen. I was excited by the idea of being able to compete without doing a flip turn in the middle of a race.

"A straight shot, gal," Dad said. "No breathing needed."

Cincinnati also offered my first experience with snow. An hour before my 50 free, my coach told me to go outside and walk around barefoot in it. Even though my freezing-cold feet felt like they were on fire, I pretended not to feel any pain. I wanted to control my reaction to discomfort the way I might have to in the race, especially if I tried to go the distance without breathing.

◆ ◆ ◆

Standing behind the blocks, I felt eerily calm. I stared down the lane with absolute certainty that I would dominate the water. The starting gun sent my fight-or-flight instincts locked in one forward motion. I never flinched, slowed, or took a breath in the twenty-nine seconds it took me to get from one end of the pool to the other.

I came out of the water exhausted *and* exhilarated. I'd broken the pool record for my age group and beaten all the racers from previous heats in addition to mine. I'd won at winning, yet again.

"Tonight we'll dine on the Ohio River," my father said when I returned to where he was standing with my coach and my mom. "A celebration on a Cincinnati riverboat!"

We supped on catfish, shrimp, and carved sirloin as the boat cruised along in the moonlight. I wore a red dress and black patent-leather shoes, with the gold medal around my neck. I was allowed my first sip of champagne when the grown-ups toasted to my victory. The bubbles gave me a feeling similar to one I got from racing—effervescence.

THE PERSIAN GULF

March 28, 2015

I open my eyes, painfully aware that it's my own D-Day. I have no antidepressants left, which means I must see a doctor for a refill as soon as possible. Allan is curled up next to me.

From our bed, I stare out the window at Abu Dhabi's shimmering sand and one of the many canals leading to the Persian Gulf. The long, narrow waterway looks a lot like the one behind my house in Florida that led to the Gulf of Mexico. I used to swim in those waters, throwing myself off the dock and racing back before an imagined shark could catch me.

I wouldn't dare swim in the waters around Mangrove Place. They're shallow and stagnant. Dr. Bercaw frequently cautioned my brother and me against entering motionless water in strange places.

"Disease lives there," he said. "You can't outswim bacteria."

Abu Dhabi's sun is just beginning to come up over the canal and desert. The orb is so big and fiery that it can't possibly be real.

I notice that the window is open even though our air conditioner is on full blast. Allan must have done it when confronted with our stale-smelling room last night. He's asked repeatedly that I rinse my wineglasses before bed and leave them in the sink. I simply choose not to comply.

In the distance, I can see a bus carrying immigrant laborers, bumping across the sand en route to Reem Island's expat enclave. All those bus passengers, and more, will spend the day cleaning our bathrooms, fixing our elevators, sweeping our parking lots, and even dangling from ropes in the sweltering heat to wash our windows.

Allan, David, and I live in the only non-glass edifice on Reem Island, which is a stone's throw from the city. If Abu Dhabi is a uterus, then Reem Island is an ovary, and the bridge between is our fallopian tube.

We picked our apartment in Mangrove Place because the price was cheaper than those in the dazzling Sun and Sky Towers across the street, but with easy access to their ground-floor shops. To get groceries, a pedicure, or a Subway sandwich, I just have to dash across a one-way four-lane road frequented by Bentleys, Maseratis, and Lamborghinis. The short journey is like a game of Pac-Man—the trick is not to get eaten by an expensive automobile.

Looking out the window in the early-morning hours, Reem Island seems like the fictional *Star Wars* planet Tatooine, with endless sand and desolation. I wouldn't be surprised if C-3PO walked over the sand dunes in the distance with his trusty sidekick, R2-D2.

And for these few precious minutes, I'm light-years away from the rest of the world. But the weight of my reality on March 28, 2015, feels like intense gravity. I have to get my medicine today, and it's going to be an ordeal—a battle with the Empire.

I'll have to take a cab to Burjeel Hospital, where I'll have to search out the general-practitioner offices. I'll have to ask if I can see a doctor about getting my prescription refilled. I've no idea what will happen next. If I don't get the meds, I'll be in bad shape within two days. No amount of booze can alleviate the withdrawal symptoms associated with abruptly ceasing antidepressants. The only things I should be going cold turkey on, I lament, are wine and vodka.

I glance down at the floor on my side of the bed and exhale loudly at the sight of the broken wineglass. *Shit,* I say under my breath, which smells stale from not brushing my teeth before bed. My tooth enamel is pitted from drinking so much wine. A month earlier, I tried to do something about my lackluster smile. But it backfired.

After receiving an email promotion for a discount on tooth whitening, I made arrangements to have the procedure. I'd tempered any anxiety about the process with the lure of looking like Julia Roberts. By the time I arrived at the dental office in a far-flung part of town, I was eager to be treated like a movie star.

But the office looked like a wasteland. The waiting-room chairs were ripped. There were no European fashion magazines on brass coffee tables. There was no brass coffee table, or any coffee table, for that matter. The wallpaper was tattered. Paint was chipped. There were no forms to sign. Nobody registered my arrival.

I entertained the notion that I'd been swindled out of $200 for a discount on something that didn't even exist. I considered walking out, but I wanted whiter teeth more than anything.

After about fifteen minutes of twiddling my thumbs—there was no Internet service, so I couldn't play with my phone—a Filipino woman in a white lab coat walked in. She escorted me to an examining room where a man was sitting at a desk behind the elevated dental chair. He instructed her, in broken English, to begin the prep. I couldn't place his accent. Italian? Egyptian? Before I could inquire, the assistant had swabbed my teeth with a heavy solution and attached an alien-looking apparatus to my face. I was pretty sure that I looked like a scuba diver in the 1950s.

"Did you read about the side effects?" the doctor called out from his chair.

Where would I have read them? How was I supposed to answer?

I couldn't even shake my head, thanks to the contraption attached to it.

"Your teeth will be porous; your gums will have white dots. Don't drink coffee or eat colorful foods for two days."

The assistant turned on a laser light inside my mouth and instructed me not to move for twenty minutes. She said we'd repeat the process three times for a total of sixty minutes. I tried to visualize time passing and my teeth whitening.

But all the while, my dentist was yelling into his phone, even smashing the receiver down. He left the room for a few minutes, slamming the door on his way out and stomping back in again a few seconds afterward.

Approximately two hundred years later, the assistant informed me that ten minutes remained in the first round. I called upon my deepest resources to stay still and sane while more screaming and yelling went on in the background. The assistant finally moved the alien apparatus aside to apply more whitening solution. Two more episodes of the procedure followed, each one seemingly taking twice as long as the previous—although they were timed at precisely twenty minutes. The phone and door slamming intensified.

The chaos happening inside and outside my mouth abruptly stopped an hour after it had begun. The dentist held up a mirror to my face so I could see the results: not Julia Roberts white, but a huge improvement. I grinned like a Cheshire cat all afternoon, eager to celebrate my winning smile with champagne in the evening.

Two days later, I was ready to reintroduce coffee into my diet, as per the dentist's instructions. Rocky, our coffee boy at work, looked relieved that I was back to drinking the Nescafé he delivered. He always seemed worried whenever I shunned my standard morning fuel. On those occasions, he brought ginger ale instead, as if he knew that I was suffering from the side effects of having drunk something else the night before.

I headed to the restroom after my first cup of coffee, pausing at the sink's mirror to admire my teeth. I screamed at the vision staring back at me. My teeth were yellow again—almost worse than before the procedure. They had soaked up the coffee like a sponge. Maybe the doctor had said two weeks, not two days. I leaned my head against the wall and fought back tears.

On the way home that evening, I instructed the cabdriver to stop at Spinneys. Inside, I bought two bottles of red wine. I decided to take my mistake as far as it would go—to win at losing.

◆　◆　◆

I ease myself out of bed, trying not to wake Allan. I need to perform like a champ today. Get my meds, get to work, get more wine, and get back home again. I start by brushing my teeth vigorously, as if I'm Lady Macbeth and dental stains are the proof of my crime.

THE JUSTUS AQUATIC
CENTER

March 14, 1986

My eighteen-year career in swimming came to a climax on the last day of the NCAA Championships in Orlando, Florida, in March 1986. My women's team from the University of South Florida led by more than 100 points, which meant the six-foot-tall championship trophy would be ours by nightfall.

But I had one more mission to accomplish that evening—qualify for the 1988 Olympic Trials in the 50-meter freestyle. The Seoul Games, still two years away, would mark the first occasion that the event would be part of the lineup. I wanted to be able to say, for the rest of my life, that I'd made history as well as the cut.

The qualifying time was set at 23.69. My personal best was 23.95. I needed to drop .26 at the Championships, in what would also be my last race before graduating from college. I hadn't let myself consider for one second what life might be like after swimming. Every fiber of my being and every waking moment for the last four years had been focused on qualifying for the Olympic Trials. There was no tomorrow, as far as I was concerned. The end of my race was the point at which the flat world ended; any ships that continued to sail would fall off.

I'd put in 6,000 to 10,000 yards a day—3.5 to 5.6 miles—six days a week for a thousand days to arrive at this moment. I'd trained my 135-pound body to bench-press 165 pounds. Whenever my coach asked for a hundred sit-ups and push-ups during dryland training, I did double in the same amount of time.

I'd even turned trips to the grocery store into a contest: getting what I needed and out of the building in less time than the previous trip. If the checkout lines proved too slow, I'd abandon the mission.

I'd also trained myself to have an orgasm in less than twenty-four seconds. I could drain a twelve-ounce beer in twenty-three seconds. Both feats were the product of my determination to be exceptional at everything, and fed my Olympic dreams.

◆ ◆ ◆

On Friday nights, our swim team gathered at a captain's apartment to celebrate another week of dominance in the water. The host bought a keg of Budweiser and we all pitched in for pizzas—dozens and dozens of them, because our appetites were as bottomless as our thirst. Someone took charge of buying and making our favorite beverage—fruit punch with pure grain alcohol. First-year swimmers, not yet at the legal drinking age, were tasked with buying ice.

We drank and danced with as much vigor as we swam with. One by one, my teammates would fall asleep, strewn across floors, couches, and each other. I liked to be the last one standing and the first one up.

On the way to Saturday morning's grueling workout, we passed around tubes of toothpaste and boxes of Tic Tacs. If a coach smelled liquor on anyone's breath, the whole team would be punished with added yardage.

Members of the swim team cast strange shadows on campus—loping around with our massive shoulders, tiny waists, and wet hair. We had far-away looks in our eyes too, which was an unintended side effect of being preoccupied with kicking and pulling, exhaling and inhaling, winning and losing, every minute of every day.

My long gaze and short shorts caught the attention of one of my professors. He invited me to his office after class one day to talk swimming.

"How did you get so fast?" he asked. "Especially at the end. Those last two seconds, when the others were losing ground."

"You went to the meet?" I asked. "I didn't see you there."

"You looked pretty focused," he answered. "I just happen to like swimming . . . and you."

We started kissing, and I ripped off my shirt. We pulled away from each other long enough to remove our pants. The whole event was over in minutes. I dressed and left the room while my professor, perhaps twenty-five years my senior, lay panting on the floor.

I swam with heightened confidence at practice that afternoon. I worked on "negative splitting," a strategy in which the second half of a race is faster than the first. Most often used by distance swimmers, negative splitting is extremely difficult for sprinters. People like me begin at top speed and battle crushing fatigue on the homestretch. Speeding up at the finish requires swimmers to tap into reserves that may be depleted, like looking for a few drops of fuel in a tank that has already run out of gas. But I was certain that I could train myself to find more even if I ran dry.

◆ ◆ ◆

Standing behind the starting blocks before my race at the National Championships, I knew that I'd done everything humanly possible to qualify for the Olympic Trials. All I had to do was unleash what was ready to burst forth.

My father was in the stands with his new wife, but I didn't scan the crowd for him. My parents had divorced during my first year at USF, at which time my dad had also relocated to Tampa. He'd taken a position as a professor of neurology at the medical school, which was located about four blocks from my dorm.

We lunched once a week to catch up on my swimming and studies, as well as his presentations at grand rounds, but we never spoke about the gaping hole his departure had left. In fact, I'd gone home almost every weekend that year to check on my mother, who was bedridden with grief. She could barely take care of my brother, who was ten at the time. Having polarized parents—a father with newfound happiness and a mother with profound sadness—meant living two separate existences. More than ever, the water became my sanctuary. The one place where I was whole and everyone else was sidelined.

When the starter blew his whistle, I stepped onto my block. The crowd went silent.

Swimmers, take your mark.

I inhaled sharply, as I bent over to grab the front of my block, and then let the air out through my nostrils. I cocked my ears to listen for the official's finger to begin its descent upon the start button. If I could detect an almost soundless sound before the buzzer went off, I might be able to cut an extra .01 seconds off my start, inching me even closer to that 23.69 qualifying time. But if I reacted too soon, I'd be charged with a false start. Victory and destruction perched on the same cliff.

Beeeeeep.

I hit the water and surfaced at full throttle. I took no breaths for the first length. I left no muscle untapped. On the way back, I found more still from which to draw. A seemingly bottomless tank.

With one yard left, I kicked as if under jet propulsion. I extended my right arm to its fullest and smashed into the wall with nearly enough force to break through the tile.

I turned to see the fluorescent numbers by my name on the black LED screen.

23.69.

THE PERSIAN GULF

March 28, 2015

From our doorway, before heading down to David's room, I turn to look at Allan sleeping peacefully. I have no idea what time he got home, but I was probably snoring up a storm by then.

Allan complains about the strange noises I make in the night. He says it sounds like I stop breathing for a few seconds before starting again. I fear that I may be suffering from sleep apnea. My father first told me about the potentially deadly disorder after I mentioned that he'd been snoring all night during a camping trip. He told me to use his Swiss Army knife to give him a tracheotomy if he ever stopped breathing altogether. He showed me exactly where—and how deep—to make the cut along his neck.

Outside David's room, I temper my rising angst about the difficult task ahead—getting my medicine—with gratitude for the clean laundry on the patio clothesline. I can look good even though I feel like shit. And David's school uniform will be crisp and ready to go. A tidy appearance is proof that he's well cared for at home.

We have a small washing machine in the kitchen, but the Abu Dhabi air serves as our clothes dryer. The whole town is one big blast of hot dry air, so there's no need for machines to do likewise. Doing laundry is a pretty simple operation, even for someone who drinks too much. Yet for our first month here, I managed to botch that process.

On my very first trip to the ginormous LuLu Hypermarket, I'd grabbed the first box of detergent in my path. I proceeded to do about ten loads of wash with the stuff, not bothering to read the English instructions next to the Arabic ones, before noticing that our clothes were stiff and our skin was rashy. I tried hanging the laundry on our bathroom towel racks instead of the clothesline on the porch. Still, they dried like scratchy cardboard.

A month later, I stood in front of the same shelves of detergents at the same LuLu and tried to decipher the situation. Every single box featured the English word *softener* and showed pictures of moms cuddling babies. Could it be that all laundry detergent in Abu Dhabi was simply referred to as *softener? Oh, the secrets of the Middle East.*

I finally settled on one that said *Eco-friendly for sensitive skin.* And then I went in search of a lunch box, thinking I'd try harder to pack fresh meals for David every day instead of letting him buy starchy food from the school canteen. I hummed a little song of my own making as I pushed my cart.

I can live in the UAE and find my way.

I cracked the laundry code.

I am the mother lode.

But a few aisles over, still humming my absurd tune, I came upon a shocking scene: shelf after shelf of detergents named Fab and All, the exact same brands found in grocery stores and homes across America. No big secret. No code to break. Detergent was detergent.

I'd been using a full cup of fabric softener to wash our clothes—four times the recommended amount, enough to have the opposite effect on our laundry. Instead of being soft and lightly perfumed, our clothes were as stiff as plaster and smelled like a nuclear explosion of roses.

"No wonder my socks were as hard as my shoes, Mommy!" David squealed when I told him about the mix-up.

Now I open his bedroom door to see my sweet boy sleeping in his soft sheets, which were washed with Tide. David is holding a stuffed polar bear we bought at the Emirates Park Zoo. We hadn't actually seen a polar bear, but the cuddly arctic animal was David's top choice as a souvenir from the gift shop. Allan and I agreed that it made sense somehow. We were the polar bears in Abu Dhabi—hot, confused, and completely out of our element.

LAKE VICTORIA

October 5, 1986

A victory *and* a loss was the contradictory outcome to my 50-freestyle race at the National Championships. I'd qualified for the Olympic Trials, but I'd also finished in second place, by .01—one-hundredth of a second—to a swimmer named Angel. And with the end of the race came the edge of my flat world. I was poised to fall off and into nothingness.

I'd earned the right to compete for a chance to be on the 1988 US Olympic Swimming Team, which meant I was also faced with the reality of training for twenty-four more months. I couldn't swim with my college team because my NCAA eligibility had run out after four years. I couldn't swim with my club team because my father had let our membership expire after the divorce. Besides, there wasn't a group for swimmers over the age of eighteen. And, to top it all off, my right shoulder was in bad shape from the inordinate amount of training I'd done to make the cut.

Graduating from college meant graduating from the sport of swimming. And only amateur athletes could compete in the Games, which meant no one could pay you to swim or train.

Even if I could find a way to keep going, the odds of making the Olympic team were against me. Dozens of younger girls in club leagues around the country were already swimming well under the cut, in addition to all the big names dominating the race in other collegiate divisions. They'd cannibalize each other for one of the two spots open to the fastest freestyle sprinters. I was being spit out of a sport that had consumed me.

When the fastest race in my life was over, so too was my time in the water. Ultimately, I'd been defeated by the time I'd worked so hard to beat. Whether I swam a 23.69 or not, this day and this conclusion were inevitable. I was washed up at age twenty.

Throwing back my second bottle of champagne that night, I made the decision to apply for the United States Peace Corps, known to be extremely selective of applicants. Being a member of their elite team would take me away from Florida and plop me down somewhere far, far away, where I could begin to craft a new version of me—a Nancy Bercaw who ruled on land.

I spent the summer after graduation teaching little kids to swim and waiting for news from the Peace Corps. In the fall of 1986, I received an official acceptance letter. And two months later, I was on a plane to Kenya with sixty other volunteers.

Kenyans, I soon discovered, pronounced my organization as "Peace Corpse." The mistake was ironic, because dying was a part of everyday life in the rural villages where volunteers were sent. In fact, my tiny town of Maragoli was home to a shop suggesting that passersby "Pop in for a Coffin." The only other store in the area offered soda pop and laundry soap. Death, Fanta, and Omo were readily available to all.

Known as one of the most densely populated places on the planet, as well as one of the oldest, Maragoli seemed to be quite literally running out of time. Bantu families in these parts had been multiplying exponentially and subdividing their farmland among their eldest male children since 1000 BC.

By the time I washed up, several millennia later, Maragoli had more people than plots. To make matters worse, the village was part of the greater Lake Victoria area known as Africa's AIDS and malaria basin. Few people in these parts lived beyond forty.

What Maragoli needed were more doctors, nurses, bioengineers, agriculture economists, animal scientists, nutritionists, crop consultants, and irrigation specialists. Instead they got me, a fish out of water.

Students walked a long way on bare feet to come to Munzatsi Friends Secondary School—five cement classrooms with tin roofs. The windows had no panes, so the afternoon rains turned the dirt floors to mud. Rickety desks and chairs and scratched-up blackboards were the only fixtures. My students each wore a turquoise polyester shirt and brown shorts, a uniform that cost their families more than they had to spare. For many, these were their only clothes.

And I had only one book from which to teach English literature. On cool mornings, we'd sit outside on top of a large gray boulder where I'd read for an hour or two. The book, titled *So Long a Letter*, was written by a Senegalese author named Mariama Bâ, and consisted of the correspondence between two West African women who were grappling with the notions of free will, fate, and feminism in Islamic society.

The subject matter perplexed my students. Maragolis had no experience whatsoever with the concept of choice. They were born poor and would likely remain so until succumbing to an early death from infectious disease. The idea of changing the course of their lives was incomprehensible. Christianity, which had replaced their pagan religion, offered the hope of something better after death.

"Read it to us again," said the eldest student, after a week of listening to me enunciate every word slowly for two hours each day. "We are not understanding."

I started over. We had no deadline, no time frame, and no other book. There was nothing else to do.

On the clearest days, from our hillside perch, we could see Lake Victoria to the west. The water there, I told my students, was the source of the Nile, which runs north, defying all expectations of a river. The water makes its way up through neighboring Uganda into Sudan and Egypt before spilling out into the Mediterranean Sea.

They stared at me as if I had two heads, with talk of water moving like a snake up through Africa. Indeed, they stared at me regardless of what I said. What a strange addition I was to their lives, with my funny clothes and freckled skin.

"Why is our madam covered in white fur?" I overheard a female student ask another.

My blonde arm hair and leg hair must have given me the appearance of a seal or polar bear. I'd shaved every hair off my limbs for the NCAA Championships, as swimmers do to reduce drag in the water, and now I considered doing so again to make myself less freakish to the Maragolis.

"Have you ever been to Lake Victoria?" I asked the class.

"No, madam," they said in unison, as if I were asking about Mount Everest, not a landmark a mere twenty kilometers away.

I didn't tell them that I made the short journey down to Kisumu every Saturday to go swimming at the Sunset Hotel on the lakeshore. While I splashed around leisurely in that pool for hours, my students carried buckets of stream water on their heads for miles.

The city of Kisumu, Kenya's third largest, didn't have much to offer tourists other than the Sunset Hotel and a pizza joint. The main draw was seeing the lake that Sir Richard Burton and John Hanning Speke had fought so hard and long to "discover" in the 1850s, even though millions of Africans had been blissfully aware of its location for thousands of years.

I made a discovery of my own in Kisumu while strolling through the city's backstreets, carefully avoiding the open sewage gutters. I heard a loud baseline beat. I could feel it in my feet, like a rumbling inside the earth.

I followed the sound until I arrived at its source: the Octopus Bottoms Up Club. A small placard under the sign said "Admission 1 Shilling," which was the equivalent of twenty-five cents in US currency and a hefty price where people earned a few dollars per week. I made $200 a month as a Peace Corps volunteer, all of which I was saving so I could go to Zanzibar on my first vacation.

I knocked on the door of the Octopus Club. A small horizontal panel slid open and a pair of big black eyes looked into my blue ones.

"*Hodi?*" I said. *May I come in?*

"*Karibu,*" the bouncer answered. *Welcome.*

"*Mzungu sawa sawa?*" I asked. *White people okay?*

"*Ndiyo,*" he laughed. *Yes.*

I gave him a shilling, and he instructed me to climb the steep, sagging stairs behind him. At the top, I walked into a room about the size of a basketball court, full of people swaying rhythmically under a giant silver disco ball.

The music playing was *dansi*, a funky African jazz. I knew it well from Kenya's local *matatu* buses, which blast dansi to lure people onboard.

Every matatu comes with a hawker, who hangs off the back door and hollers for passengers to come along for the ride.

"*Hapa!*" they scream. *Here!*

The matatu in which I went from Maragoli to Kisumu and back again had bench seating for twelve people but held at least two dozen more. The exterior was slathered with red and black graffiti. And the phrase "No Harry in Africa" was scrawled across the back, where the hawker did his hawking.

Sitting six inches away from him on my first ride in "Harry," I noticed that the hawker suffered from severe elephantiasis in his left leg, which had swollen it to four times the size of his right one. Yet he didn't seem to mind the added weight and girth. He gyrated effortlessly, even seductively, to the eardrum-crushing sounds of dansi music blaring from "Harry."

The same sounds were pulsating inside the Octopus Club when I entered. I stayed near the outside walls, where posters of Bob Marley, Michael Jackson, and Stevie Wonder had been haphazardly thumb-tacked. An open window was letting in more mosquitoes than breeze. The dance floor was throwing off heat like a stove top, and I imagined that the dancers were being cooked alive like lobsters. Body odor and the smell of stale beer permeated the packed room.

But not one of the two hundred or so Kenyans in motion seemed to care. I tried to mimic their moves, swaying my girlish hips like the robust mamas around me. They smiled at my efforts and grabbed my hands to join in.

A few minutes later, the music abruptly stopped. I looked at the stage to see if there'd been a power outage, common in those parts, especially after seven p.m. But the DJ remained lit by an overhead bulb and was waving his hands.

"Dance contest!" he yelled into the microphone. "Register with the bartender! Winner gets a lifetime pass to the Octopus Club. Four more will get a year membership! Ten minutes to sign up! *Fanya huraka, mabibi na mabawna!* Hurry now, ladies and gentlemen!"

I made my way to the bar, passing groups of dancers in conversation about who would enter the contest and who should win. Few people paid any attention to the *mzungu* in their midst—my whiteness more of an eyesore than some latent colonialist threat.

I signed up for the dance contest and bought the largest-sized bottle of Tusker beer. I wrote my name next to Prince's song "Let's Go Crazy" on the list of available music.

"Maybe I'll win," I told the bartender. He laughed and handed me a Sportsman cigarette from his own pack. I'd taken up smoking since I'd quit swimming, joking that my lungs were bored without the challenge of inhaling and exhaling in the pool. I liked the little extra buzz cigarettes provided.

Contestants were called by name, one at a time, to dance on the small stage. The crowd went crazy for Titus, a very slender fellow in a dark-brown suit with moves like Michael Jackson's. Next came a voluptuous woman with undulating hips and big bouncing breasts. We chanted her name—"Abuya! Abuya! Abuya!"—in time with her sensual choreography. Compared to Abuya, I was a poor excuse for a woman—rail thin and flat chested. My female students had expressed concern over my ability to have a baby. In their opinion, I should have had two or three by now.

The DJ hyperpronounced my name: "Nan-see Bird-cow."

I got cheers, catcalls, and whistles. But everyone quieted down when I was onstage and Prince's music started building momentum through the speakers. I danced slowly at first, picking up speed as the music did. By the end, I was jumping and twirling, swinging my long blonde hair like a mop. I did a midair split, landing on my feet.

When Prince and I were done, the crowd hooted and hollered with as much enthusiasm as I had danced with. Some people chanted my name: *Nan-see. Nan-see. Nan-see.*

I got high fives and handshakes as I made my way back to the bar for a beer, which the bartender handed over free of charge.

"You dance like Maasai warrior," he said, referring to the tribe of tall, lean people in southern Kenya, famous for their jumping dances.

I chugged the beer as sweat poured down my face, T-shirt, and skirt. Even my old sneakers got damp. People continued to congratulate me while the contest raged on.

"Mzuri sana, bibi!" Very good, girl.

As soon as my beer was empty, I was presented with another. When that one ran dry, another appeared before me. If I'd had eight arms, someone at the Octopus Club would have made sure a Tusker beer or a Sportsman cigarette was in each hand.

Shortly after midnight, the DJ stopped the music to announce the winners, explaining that he was the lone voter and had gauged his choices by creativity, technique, and crowd response.

"In fifth place . . . Abuya!" Cheers echoed off the walls as she took the stage and received her certificate.

The DJ announced fourth and third places, screams of support reaching down to the lake basin and echoing back to the Octopus.

"And in second place," the DJ boomed, "Nan-see! *Maridadi mwalimu* from Maragoli!" He'd called me a beautiful teacher. I hesitated before taking the stage, unsure of my own description.

Abuya embraced me. The DJ put Prince's record back on, and everyone in the Octopus Club started jumping as I had done in my performance. Some going up. Others coming down. The room moving like a choppy ocean wake.

Beer in hand, I stared out across the frenzied Octopus Club at the sea of Kenyans teaching me how to navigate existence on their land, not vice versa.

"Kwa maisha!" I said, lifting my beer and taking a swig. *To life!*

THE PERSIAN GULF

March 28, 2015

I ease into the shower. The warm water clears my head enough to think about the battle ahead: middle-aged American woman versus the Middle East. Will I get my pills or a kick in the butt? I fear that I am the kind of expat Abu Dhabi doesn't want or need. Maybe the doctor will recommend I leave his office and the country.

Drying off, I draw a heart in the fogged-up mirror and write my son's name inside it. I study my image as the fog clears. The desert and the drinking have aged me. My features look lost on my face. Gone are the high, well-defined cheekbones of my glory days. My eyes look like I've been swimming in an overchlorinated pool without goggles. I reach for the Visine and notice the bottle is as empty as my antidepressant bottle.

My stomach cramps up, and I'm glad to be one quick step from the toilet, with my pants already off. I need to be near a restroom at all times because my sphincter muscles have all but given up holding in my chronic diarrhea.

The problem comes into play wherever I go, usually at the most inopportune times. A month earlier, it hit in the middle of nowhere as David and I headed to Al Ain, in eastern Abu Dhabi, to visit my friend Simi and her family. I first met Simi, a British citizen of Indian descent, a few months after we arrived. She was at the British Club visiting our mutual friend Abbi. Their two families were sitting out in the shallow Gulf waters where David and I were looking for shells. Abbi introduced us and I knew, based on Simi's big smile and wild laugh, that she'd be my friend for life.

On the long stretch of highway between Abu Dhabi and Al Ain, where camels ride in the backs of pickup trucks, there are only a handful of refueling stops. When my stomach started rumbling, I asked our driver, Durminder, to pull over at the nearest possible petrol station, which turned out to be only a kilometer away. His English wasn't particularly good, but we managed to communicate nonetheless. Simi knew him from Al Ain and had hired him to retrieve us in Abu Dhabi and bring us to her house.

Durminder referred to David as "baby." Perhaps he was longing for a baby of his own, since, as Simi said, he was heading home to Sri Lanka soon to marry his girlfriend. At the petrol station, I said, "Baby stay," to indicate that David should wait in the car with Durminder.

I walked quickly to the women's bathroom and into one of the two stalls, taking note of an elderly Indian woman sitting on an old school chair in the corner. She was crying into her cell phone and speaking softly. The sound of her suffering made my stomach spasm even more.

I washed my hands at the sink and pushed the button of the hand dryer, which didn't start. I tried again, wishing it would muffle the sounds of the woman's wails. Staring at the useless machine, I felt a light touch on my shoulder. The elderly Indian woman, who still had the phone to her ear, was handing me a roll of toilet paper with which to dry my hands. Tears were streaming down the deep crevices in her face.

She was the restroom attendant—making sure I could dry my hands even though she was in the midst of a personal crisis. I used a piece of the toilet paper to dab at her tears. She grabbed my hand with her free one and clung to me tightly. We held on to each other as if we were being taken out by a rip current—the wet tissue between our palms like a tiny little life preserver.

I hated to let go, after witnessing the depths of her grief, but I wanted to get back to my child. The elderly woman returned to her chair in the corner and continued to cry.

In the backseat of Durminder's car, I told David about the sad woman in the bathroom and that I was sad as a result of meeting her. He reached for my hand.

Now, getting up from the toilet in our apartment, I decide to shower again. Whatever has come out of me smelled like the contents of the hole in the ground where I defecated in Kenya. I want to feel fresh and clean when I go in search of my medication later.

I put on a pair of black pants and my long-sleeved leopard-print blouse. No matter what I wear, I'll be overheated. I slip on my four-inch platform sandals. They exaggerate my height, which helps minimize my girth, or so I believe.

After David eats breakfast, I walk him across the street to catch his bus for the American International School. We see the window washers, dressed in bright-orange jumpsuits, as they scale across the face of Sun and Sky Towers' seventy-four floors. The workers aren't standing on scaffolding like window washers in New York City; they're dangling from ropes and pulleys. They're using their feet to walk perpendicular to the ground.

"Those are the real Spider-Men," David says. I reach one of my arms around his shoulders and pull him in tight. *This kid is the hero,* I tell myself. He endures my never-ending need to be elsewhere, my unwavering desire to race back and forth across experiences like laps in a swimming pool.

I catch a glimpse of my reflection in the clean windows on the ground floor. I look pregnant, even though that's not possible. I haven't had a period in two years. I haven't had sex in two months. Is it the angle of the reflection? Or an optical illusion created by a slight bend in the glass? I couldn't possibly be so disproportionate around the middle. I look at the other mothers gathered around and check their reflections in the glass. They look the same in both places: fit and trim. *It's the angle,* I tell myself again, *like a fun-house mirror at a county fair. I'm just standing in the wrong place.*

The bus stop looks like a scene from the United Nations Office at Geneva. Kids of all nationalities in neatly pressed uniforms are bound for institutions named for their native countries: the Canadian International School, the British School, Indian School, the Australian School. All of their institutions advertised in big black letters on their yellow buses.

Except for David's bus, I suddenly realize even though I've had this same routine for months. The only designation on the American School bus is a small placard in the front window with the number 7. Reality hits me like a derailed train: my son and his fellow students are being protected from anti-Americanism and terrorism. If something happened to David because we came to Abu Dhabi, I'd jump from the top of Sun and Sky Towers. I kiss him at least a dozen times as he gets on board.

"Wear your seatbelt!" I yell. School buses in Abu Dhabi offer lap belts, unlike American buses.

When his unmarked bus pulls away, I study the Spider-Men nearing the highest heights. Do they ever come crashing down? If so, we never hear about it. But the image of myself in their clean windows clearly shows just how far I've fallen.

THE INDIAN OCEAN

March 20, 1987

Inside the tiny and sparse Kenya Airways office in Kisumu, I purchased a round-trip plane ticket to Zanzibar for a hundred dollars. I had another hundred to spend on lodging, meals, and drink. Other Peace Corps volunteers who'd visited the island had given me the names of cheap guesthouses and said I could easily last a week on a hundred dollars or less.

I took the overnight train to Nairobi to catch my afternoon flight. I wasn't sure how readily available alcohol would be on a predominantly Muslim island, so I bought a bottle of scotch at the duty-free shop in Jomo Kenyatta Airport. With ninety dollars in my pocket, a black string bikini, and a fifth of Johnnie Walker Red in my backpack, I boarded the plane.

I landed ninety minutes later in Dar es Salaam, Tanzania, in plenty of time to make my connection to Zanzibar, a short hop over a small stretch of the Indian Ocean. I was perplexed by the word "canceled" next to my flight number on the departure screen. I scanned down for the next flight, only to find that it had been canceled as well. A few other passengers shrugged and walked away.

I found an Air Tanzania agent at a nearby gate. The airport was a ghost town. I half expected tumbleweed to roll down the barren terminal.

"Zanzibar is canceled?" I asked.

She nodded. "For a few days. Maybe a week. Tarmac closed for repair."

"Can I take a ferry or something?"

"No boats, either."

"The port is under repair?" I asked, not intending to sound flippant. It was a legitimate question in a part of the world fraught with chaos. So much of Tanzania's infrastructure was in disrepair that authorities had difficulty prioritizing the work.

The agent shrugged and went back to staring at her computer. Canceled flights, closed-down countries, broken planes were each just another blip on her radar screen.

I wouldn't get to Zanzibar unless I swam over. But the seventy-four-kilometer distance was far too much for a sprinter. Besides, the deep waters in between were infested with man-of-war jellyfish and great white sharks—sea snakes too, with a far more venomous bite than the cottonmouth moccasins back in the Alabama river where my dad had taught me to swim.

"Can I return to Nairobi?" I asked the agent.

"Ticket date?"

"A week from today."

"You can go that day," she said, looking back at her screen.

"There's no standby list?" I pleaded.

"You can stand here," she said without the slightest trace of sarcasm. She was giving me permission to hang out at the gate for a week. There was no list, of any kind, for anything.

"*Asante,*" I said. *Thank you.*

I left to explore a city I'd been warned not to visit. Dar was notorious for two things: corruption and crime. It was considered the wild, wild West of East Africa, complete with urban cowboys and arms dealers, and everything in Dar was up for grabs—especially backpacks and the foreign women carrying them.

I decided to find the city's finest hotel and blow most of my funds on a night of dinner and drinks. I'd take a bus back to Nairobi in the morning.

A cabdriver dropped me off at the Kilimanjaro Hotel, reportedly the best in town. When we pulled up, the Kilimanjaro looked more like an abandoned fallout shelter from the fifties than the beautiful mountain for which it was named. The boxy building was partially obstructed by overgrown brush, and the green-tinted glass windows were covered in thick dust.

I asked the front-desk clerk for the least expensive room for one night, which he gave me for seventy-five US dollars and the privilege of putting a five-dollar gratuity in his pocket. A forlorn bellhop in a tattered blue uniform and sandals made from the rubber of an old tire escorted me in the elevator to the sixth floor. He offered to carry my backpack but seemed relieved when I said no. I tipped him a shilling for accompanying me and for pointing out the shampoos in the bathroom.

Standing on the lime-green shag carpet in my room, I looked out the window for the Indian Ocean. But the view I had was toward the center of town. I watched as dusk descended and a handful of attractive buildings lit up. Like Kisumu, Dar had limited hours of electricity. Wealthy residents got first dibs.

I took a long, hot shower and used the entire contents of the small Breck shampoo bottle. I had no electricity or running water in Maragoli. But I did have a rain tank, the contents of which were protected by a padlock. Every evening, I released enough water to wash my underwear, my cup and dish, and my armpits in the same small basin.

My toilet in Maragoli was a hole in the ground, located in a wood-shed a few steps away from my thatched-roof cement house. After witnessing a black mamba snake slither from the outhouse, I'd started doing my business behind a boulder at the edge of the hill in my back-yard. Toilet paper was nonexistent in Maragoli. There wasn't even a name for it, until I invented one at the tiny *duka* shop selling detergent and orange soda.

"*Karatasi ya choo?*" Paper of the toilet?

The proprietor laughed so violently she knocked over her display of two empty soda bottles. My lightning reflexes caught both before they could hit the ground—a sight that caused the shopkeeper's eyes to get big as saucers. She hissed and shooed me away as if I were a witch.

After lathering from head to toe in the Kilimanjaro, I felt clean for the first time in months. I liked having a towel around my waist again and the sensation of a soft bath mat under my feet. I took the blow-dryer off the wall and proceeded to make my hair as fluffy and feathered as Farrah Fawcett's locks.

I put on the white blouse and dark-blue Levi's that I'd hand washed and dried on a rock before leaving Maragoli. I briefly wished for fancier shoes than my beaded sandals before heading downstairs to the Flame Tree Lounge in the hotel lobby. But I consoled myself with the fact that my feet were clean.

I ordered an icy glass of cheap whiskey from the bartender and lifted a copy of the local newspaper off the bar top. I scanned for any news of Zanzibar's imminent reopening.

"Can I buy you that drink?"

I looked up to see a middle-aged Indian man in a well-cut suit standing at my side.

"Sure."

He sat down on the opposite stool after introducing himself as Rashid.

"What are you doing here?" he asked.

I told him the story of Zanzibar's closing, my hut in rural Kenya, and my dwindling funds. He insisted that I be his dinner guest. He was a visitor there too, from New Delhi, exploring the idea of opening a restaurant in Dar. A great number of Indians called East Africa home, he said. I told him how I'd met some of his countrymen in Nairobi and Kisumu. They always wanted to feed me, and I appreciated their generosity.

We took our drinks to the restaurant at the top of the hotel. The floor-to-ceiling windows offered a panoramic view of Dar, which was lit up like a Christmas tree with a bunch of broken bulbs. The Indian Ocean shimmered in the distance.

When Rashid poured me a glass of Riesling from the bottle he'd ordered, I tried to remain calm. I'd been drinking warm beer for months and craved the cool, crisp liquid that would bring me back to life.

Rashid and I talked about the poverty in his country and the lasting effects of India's partition with Pakistan. I told him about living near the border of Uganda and how territorial skirmishes lingered between the people who'd been divided by the line. The British, we agreed, had no business mapping out these places, yet they'd done so anyway.

Rashid reached his hand out to touch mine. I withdrew, putting my hands in my lap. He clearly wanted a return on his dinner investment, but I wasn't interested in paying up. When he excused himself to use the restroom, I looked around for an exit strategy.

I noticed four European men at a neighboring table. One of them was so handsome that he took my breath away—a cigarette dangling from the full lips on his tan face, a wild mop of brown hair like a lion's mane.

I asked the waiter for a pen and a piece of paper.

Save me, I wrote.

I watched as the waiter delivered it to a man who looked like he'd stepped out of an Ernest Hemingway novel or a George Michael MTV video. A huge lion claw hung from a thick gold chain around his neck.

Game hunter, I imagined. He wore gold elephant-hair bracelets on both wrists.

After glancing at my note, he stood up. But instead of coming in my direction, he made a beeline for the restroom. Defeated, I gulped the last of my wine. The meal hadn't even arrived yet, but I was ready to call it a night. Coming to Tanzania had been a mistake. I'd drink the error away with the whiskey in my room.

Rashid, looking ashen, returned accompanied by the object of my affection from the other table. Rashid politely said that he needed to leave and suggested that I enjoy dinner with the other young people. He walked away quickly, never glancing back.

"You're free," said the young man in a heavy accent.

"Where are you from?" I asked. "What's your name?"

"Turkey. I'm Cemal."

I imagined that we'd live in Dar happily ever after. We'd honeymoon in Zanzibar. Our children would grow up speaking Swahili and running wild.

"Come," he said, reaching for my hand.

Cemal walked me to his table and gave me his seat. He took the chair from another table and tucked himself in next to me.

He ordered another bottle of wine for me and resumed his conversation in Turkish with the other men. I chain-smoked his cigarettes and listened to their colorful language. I stared at Cemal as he spoke and put my hand on his knee under the table.

Over dinner, one of the other men—all of whom spoke English fairly well—asked what a young American woman was doing alone in Dar. I told them the whole story, including my years as a swimmer and my recent victory at the Octopus Club. I concluded with my current predicament, since Zanzibar was closed and my funds were depleted.

"Stay with me," Cemal said. The other men nodded in approval. After several rounds of after-dinner drinks, the group dispersed. Cemal walked me to my room, where I pulled him inside and onto one of the twin beds. We devoured each other from head to toe, with remarkable speed. I couldn't get enough of him, fast enough. He was a sprinter too.

◆ ◆ ◆

In the morning light, Cemal traced the freckles on my back.

"Nice decorations," he said, taking the gold lion claw off his neck and putting it around mine.

"Wait for me here," he instructed. "Don't leave the hotel. Dangerous outside."

I went back to sleep. He called at noon and told me to pack up and meet him in the lobby.

Cemal helped me into the front seat of his Land Rover. An elderly lady greeted me in Turkish from the backseat.

"My grandmother," Cemal said, smiling. He handed me a pack of cigarettes, and one back to her. She hummed a tune, directing an invisible orchestra with her lighted smoke. Granny's black hair was pulled back and covered with a peach scarf. She appeared to be in her mid-seventies, with deep wrinkles around her eyes. In her lovely and loose pink dress, she sat low in the backseat. I guessed she was at least a foot shorter than Cemal, who was six feet tall.

Granny seemed nonchalant at my arrival on the scene. She was happy to travel anywhere with her handsome grandson, as was I. Cemal said she'd come all the way from Istanbul to spend time with him. She seemed as adventurous as us.

"Where are we going?" I asked. My thighs were sore. Rug burns on my back. I hoped there was a pool at our destination. The chlorine would heal me before new wounds could be made.

"Mikumi National Park, Morogoro," he said. "I have business there."

"Safari business?"

"Restaurant business."

I was relieved that Cemal wasn't a hunter, or in the Turkish mafia, as I'd also begun to suspect. He was a twenty-seven-year-old entrepreneur in Tanzania in search of financial opportunities, not big game.

Our unlikely trio arrived at Morogoro just before nightfall. Granny got her own suite; Cemal and I were in another. For the next three days, Granny and I hung out by the pool while our boy attended to business. A monkey swooped down on our picnic table during lunch on the second day and stole Granny's sandwich right out of her hands. After we stopped yelling obscenities in Turkish and English, Granny and I laughed like the hyenas we'd seen on the previous day's safari through Mikumi National Park.

We lavishly dined with Cemal and his business partners in the evenings. We started with cocktails in the hotel bar and ended with after-dinner drinks on the front porch, the rising African moon above us.

With three days left before my flight to Kenya, we headed back to Dar. Cemal dropped Granny off at his house before checking us back into the Kilimanjaro. We made love all day and drank all night for forty-eight hours. Whiskey helped slow the passage of time. But sober, in the mornings, I was painfully aware of the seconds as I was losing them.

On my last night in Tanzania, we retrieved Granny and made our way to a mosque. Instead of saying prayers, we'd come to play bingo with a hundred or so local and expat Muslims. I covered my head with a scarf Granny provided, in keeping with female custom.

I tried to imagine what it would be like to marry Cemal. I'd have to convert. We'd settle into traditional roles. I'd be relegated to the women's room at social gatherings, apart from the men. Everything wild and free in me would be tamed; my liberator would become my captor.

I neutralized my angst with shots of scotch during long breaks when many of the male players went outside to smoke and drink. I was surprised to see just how many of the devout actually imbibed. I figured this wasn't the case in other parts of the Muslim world. In Tanzania, I assumed, anything goes.

Toward the end of the evening, I switched my focus from drinking to the five bingo cards laid out in front of me. To win the grand prize of 50,000 Tanzanian shillings, every space on one of the boards had to be covered by a chip. No empty spots whatsoever. Winning the money would help me build a library at Munzatsi Secondary School. A rush of adrenaline came over me.

"Forty-two!" the caller announced in English through a scratchy sound system. Then again in Arabic: *"Ithnan wa-arba'un."* A third time in Swahili: *"Arobaini na mbili."*

I moved a chip over the last open number on one of my cards. Double-, then triple-checking that it was, in fact, 42.

"Bingo!" I yelled. "Bingo!"

"Jesus H. Christ!" I blurted out to Cemal, who laughed at my choice of expression in a mosque. "I won! I won!"

He whispered in my ear that I should split my prize money with the man who'd provided me with the winning card.

"The dealer?" I asked, getting up from our folding table to collect my winnings from the stage.

Cemal nodded, and I resisted the urge to kiss him in front of God and everyone. I walked barefoot to the front of the room over a path of overlapping Turkish carpets. The crowd clapped enthusiastically. I waved as if I were an Olympic champion headed to the podium to collect my gold medal.

Cemal and I didn't make love that night. We lay in bed, guzzling whiskey from plastic cups and smoking. When Cemal finally fell asleep, I kept drinking. Being drunk gave me power over time just as swimming once had. Yet time, and booze, would run out, as they always did.

THE PERSIAN GULF

March 28, 2015

I tell the cabdriver to take me to Burjeel Hospital. He starts weaving in and out of traffic on Abu Dhabi's Salaam Street, accelerating toward the bumpers of other commuters before slamming on his brakes. I'm in the opposite of a hurry. I want time to go backward. In fact, I *don't* want to get where I'm going. I'd much rather be in a Kenyan matatu where the journey is more important than the destination.

"No hurry," I tell him. "We'll get there when we get there."

"Insha'Allah," he answers.

Insha'Allah is everyone's mantra in Abu Dhabi, just as it was in Kenya and Tanzania. *God willing.*

I ask my cabdriver from where he hails. He appears to be African, and the nameplate above his meter says *Francis.* Could be from anywhere on the continent, I surmise.

"Kenya," he answers.

"Jambo, bwana!"

I excitedly tell him that I lived in his country nearly thirty years ago, which must have been at least five years before he was born. Francis looks twenty-five, roughly half my age.

"*Natoka wapi katika Kenya?*" I ask. *Which place in Kenya?*

"Maragoli."

"*Mimi pia! Me too!*" I am so elated that I briefly forget where I'm going and why. Someone from Maragoli has left the village for work elsewhere, which feels like a victory for Maragoli *and* me.

The serendipity of meeting Francis seems like a good omen. I'll get my pills and a clean bill of health. Over and out. Finished and done. *Kwisha*, in Swahili. God, it appears, is willing today.

"God is great," I tell Francis, who nods vehemently.

But I don't feel great. I feel awful. My hands are trembling. My stomach is in knots. I probably have an ulcer, or worse. I pray that it's a parasite from my days in Kenya—something for which I can take another pill.

Francis drops me at the main doors of Burjeel Hospital. I'm familiar with the building and offices, having brought David to see a pediatrician for a tummy ache on one occasion and a nasty cough on another. I check the directory in the lobby for the room number of general practitioners. I take the elevator to the third floor.

"Hello and good morning," I say nonchalantly to the Filipina receptionist. "I need to see a doctor about getting a prescription refilled."

"What is the name of the medicine?" she asks.

I lower my voice so the five other patients in the waiting room won't hear.

"Celexa."

"What is it for?" she asks, unfamiliar with the brand name.

"Depression," I whisper.

She crumples her brow. "I'm not sure if our doctors can prescribe that, let me check."

"You have to help me," I say urgently as she turns to leave. "I'm from the Philippines too. I was born at Clark Air Base in Pampanga. My father was a surgeon there during the Vietnam War."

She smiles and walks away. I hope she'll advocate for her fellow countrywoman. But rules are rules in Abu Dhabi.

Rather than take a seat, I cling tightly to the reception desk. Between anxiety and nausea, I feel like I may pass out. I take a long, slow inhale through my nose and expel an equally long exhale through my mouth—just as I had on the starting blocks before my Olympic Trial–qualifying race.

In the water, swimmers exhale for much longer than they inhale, taking a small gulp of air every few strokes and then blowing it out continuously before breathing again. Swimmers work to increase their lung capacity through hypoxic training—only breathing every five or seven strokes or doing an entire lap underwater without coming up for air.

Going hypoxic raises carbon-dioxide levels in the bloodstream and leads to extreme discomfort. But by learning to relax instead of panic in these conditions, swimmers can stay calm even when oxygen is depleted.

I hold my breath when I see the receptionist returning. Has a doctor agreed to see me and prescribe my medicine? If so, will he or she take note of my puffy face, increased pulse, and belly fat?

"We're all set," the receptionist says. "Follow me so the nurse can check your vitals."

I have an early lead in the race to get the day over and done. A congratulatory bottle of champagne is in order if I come out on top in the end.

THE SUNSET HOTEL POOL

March 1987

Cemal and I halfheartedly agreed not to try to sustain our relationship at a distance of 1,200 kilometers. He was starting a business; I had an obligation to my village. Over many rounds of late-night whiskey, we'd allowed ourselves to fantasize about a life together. But over coffee every morning we were faced with the reality that being a long-term couple was impossible. We were from two different worlds, living in two different countries. There was Mount Kilimanjaro, and so much more, standing between us.

"What would your father think of me?" Cemal asked as we danced to George Michael's song "Careless Whisper" in our hotel room. He'd returned with his boom box after checking on his grandmother. She'd been baking and sent a box of Turkish delight back for me.

"Let's call him," I said.

Cemal gave a half smile, a sign that he was up for an adventure. He'd made the same expression upon receiving my note at the restaurant.

The hotel operator, after asking for 500 shillings to be delivered to her in a brown envelope, put me through to my dad's home number. The time was three a.m. in Florida. He answered, probably thinking it was the hospital calling to get his opinion on a patient.

"Hi, Dad! I'm in Tanzania! Don't worry; everything is fine. I'm just on vacation."

"Gal, that's great. Glad you're seeing as many places as possible. Remember to use bug spray. Malaria kills a million people a year."

"Dad, I met a man here. Maybe I'll marry him one day. He's Turkish. A Muslim. What would you think about that?"

"Gal, you have my blessing. But here's my request: if you aren't his first wife, make sure you're his best wife."

"Okay, Dad, thanks," I said, giggling. "I'll write when I'm back in Kenya in a few days. I love you."

"Your old dad loves you," he said in the third person, as he always did.

I hung up and told Cemal what Dr. Bercaw had said.

We fell down on the floor laughing in our own delight.

"I like your dad," Cemal said. "But tell him Turks only have one wife."

We didn't laugh two days later when Cemal drove me to the airport. In fact, I cried the whole way, and wept even harder when Grandma started sobbing. Cemal stared straight ahead with an unlit cigarette dangling from his mouth. At the terminal, I told him not to park and to let me out at the drop-off. Pale and teary, he nodded.

Nakupenda, I said in Swahili. *Seni seviyorum,* in Turkish. *I love you.*

Cemal put his head down on the steering wheel before driving away. I saw his bracelet-clad arm wave out the window as his Land Rover pulled into the exit lane.

I walked into the airport with his lion-claw necklace clenched in my hand, having removed it from my neck with the intention of giving it back. I'd changed my mind upon realizing the necklace was all I'd ever have of Cemal.

After the short flight to Nairobi and then the long overnight train ride to Kisumu, I decided to go to the Sunset Hotel instead of taking a matatu back to Maragoli. I needed time and space in the forms of water and wine.

In the months that I'd been swimming at the Sunset, I'd become friends with the waiter who served poolside drinks. When he told me his full name was Wilson Nixon System Odinga, I asked why his parents had used the words *Nixon* and *System*. He shrugged. When I told him my name was Nancy Stearns Bercaw, he laughed out loud.

"Stern?" he joked. *"Hii ni nini?" What is that?*

Odinga decided to refer to me as "madam," and I chose to call him by his last name. We conversed in Swahili even though he was a Luo, and his people preferred their own tribal language to the tongue of the Swahili people on the coast and the Arab traders who landed on those shores.

Luo is a Nilotic language—meaning *of the Nile*—and spoken by more than four million descendants from the riverbed region, including parts of Sudan. Spoken in a singsongy fashion, Swahili proved easy for me to learn. Luo was more complicated and sounded harsher, as most words ended in a consonant. Nearly every word in Swahili ended with a vowel.

Reclining on a lounge chair in my bikini, I waited for Odinga to come poolside, as he always did within minutes of my arrival. But when there was no sign of him after fifteen minutes, I wrapped a towel around my waist and headed up the stone path toward the main hotel.

Halfway up the hill, I saw the entire hotel staff squatting on the lawn. They looked like they were frantically weeding the grass by hand. A swarm of flies hung in the air above them. I worried that the swarm might actually be mosquitoes and their odds of getting malaria had just tripled. But it was noon, and mosquitoes didn't descend until dusk.

Odinga called to me. "Madam, *kuja hapa! Haraka!*" He was instructing me to come quickly.

I ran to him.

"*Sawa sawa?*" I asked. *Everything okay?*

"*Ndiyo,*" he exclaimed, a mouthful of something. *Yes!*

"*Nafanya nini?*" *What are you doing?*

"*Kula!*" he said. *Eat!*

I watched as Odinga and the others grabbed termites hatching from the ground, ripped off their wings, and shoved the remainders of the live insects into their mouths. Not unlike an oyster-shucking party on Cape Cod.

I sat down next to Odinga to soak in his enthusiasm and observe his technique. He was averaging fifteen termites a minute, one every four seconds. He paused briefly to hand me one, ready for consumption.

"*Kula,* madam!" *Eat!*

I swallowed the bug whole, afraid of chewing. Odinga shook his head. He showed me how he used his molars to deliver the fatal blow, then four or five quick chomps to maximize flavor prior to swallowing.

I followed suit, noting that Odinga and the others were increasing their eating speed. The termite count was tapering off—a life cycle having run its course in the blink of an eye.

By the time I had eaten three, the event was over and done. I lay down on the lawn, stunned. Odinga walked away and returned.

"*Hapa.*" He'd brought me a beer. *Here.*

I walked back to the pool, where a European man had settled into a lounge chair next to mine. He'd taken off his shoes and rolled his jeans up to the knees. His legs were gangly and his skin extremely pale. He seemed to be about my age, maybe a few years older.

"Want some of my sunscreen?" I asked.

"Ah, yes, thanks much," he said with an Irish accent. "Enjoy the annual delicacy, did you?"

"Is that what it was?"

"Very special occasion," he said. "Good of you to participate."

He said his name was Paul, after I introduced myself as a Peace Corps volunteer in the area. I asked what he was doing in Kisumu at the Sunset Hotel.

"I decided to take a long ride on my *pikipiki*."

"You have a motorbike?" I was excited to hear it, hoping for a ride back to Maragoli, if he was headed in that direction. Squishing into a loud matatu after riding around in Cemal's Land Rover was unappealing at best.

"Yes, of course. I need it for my work," he said.

"Let me guess. Water engineer."

"Strike one."

"Médecins Sans Frontières?"

"Strike two."

"Tell me already."

"Priest. Jesuit."

"Where's your collar?" I was incensed that he wasn't in uniform. Or whatever they called it. Seemed like false advertising for a priest to walk around in sheep's clothing.

"I'm off duty." He ordered a Tusker from Odinga.

I nodded to Odinga to bring me another as well and gave him the thumbs-up.

Suntanning and conversing, Paul and I each drank four beers and smoked an entire pack of cigarettes. I told him about teaching with one book in Maragoli and my accidental vacation in Dar es Salaam that ended in three broken hearts.

"Three?" he said, looking concerned that I'd been part of a seedy love triangle.

"A girl, a boy, and his grandmother," I said, trying hard not to cry.

I challenged Paul to a swim race.

"Down and back," I said. "Loser buys whiskey shots."

I could tell by the sun's position in the sky that it was already three in the afternoon. Sunrise and sunset were punctual on the equator. I wanted to be back in Maragoli by five p.m. so I could write Cemal a letter before darkness fell at six. I feared the loneliness waiting in my house. I had few candles left to light. I was tempted to go to the Octopus Club and dance off my angst, but I had to teach in the morning.

Paul unbuttoned and removed his dress shirt. I dropped my towel and walked across the deck in my bikini. He followed, still wearing his rolled-up trousers.

"You gonna swim in those things?" I asked. "They'll drag you down."

"The only way you'll beat me. I swam on the team in high school, little girl."

"Did you?" I pretended to be impressed. "Then let's get on with it. Ready, set, go!"

I was in the water before Paul even realized the race had started. I finished the second length before he'd completed the first. My rival was breathless and astonished when he reached the wall.

"I swam in college," I said.

We shook hands, like good sports. In perfect Luo, Paul asked Odinga to deliver two shots of cheap whiskey to us on the pool steps.

"You speak Luo."

"Yes, and Luhya. I give sermons in Luhya up in Bungoma, where I live and work."

"I'd like to hear you talk about God in Luhya," I said. "I could use a little saving myself."

"Why don't I drive you back to Maragoli in a little while, and then come get you next Saturday? You can be a guest in the rectory and come to services in the morning."

"That sounds fantastic. I can stay there? With priests around?"

Paul chuckled. "We have a special wing for guests. And we've been known to have female friends, even bikini-clad ones."

We clinked the whiskey shots Odinga delivered to us. "Cheers!" Odinga looked at me and said, "You're drinking too much, madam." *"Hakuna shida, rafiki,"* I answered. *There's no problem, friend.*

I wondered what Paul said to some of the world's poorest people, like Odinga, from his Sunday pulpit. From what I'd seen over the course of six months, maintaining faith in God was difficult. Life in Kenya was spectacularly unfair. And the people of Western Province had a lifespan of fifty-eight years—about three shorter than the already-disturbing national average. Someone like Odinga would likely succumb to malaria, diarrhea, TB, or HIV before reaching middle age. Maybe he'd leave a dozen children behind. Maybe his wife would predecease him in childbirth. Maybe they'd all be killed in a fiery matatu accident.

Paul drank a cup of coffee to sober up for the drive home. We smoked one last cigarette before hopping on his *piki* for the twenty-minute ride into the Maragoli hills. I felt strange wrapping my arms around a priest's waist, but even in my tipsy state I managed to find a place for my hands above his belt.

I was back in my house with plenty of time to write Cemal before darkness descended. But the full bottle of whiskey still in my backpack was calling my name. I crawled under my mosquito netting with Johnnie Walker to start the process of forgetting.

A week later, Saturday afternoon, Paul arrived at Munzatsi Secondary School and knocked on my front door. He waited outside while I finished packing for the journey. I looked around my room for a gift for my hosts, not entirely sure whom that might be. Who was Paul's boss? A deacon? I knew very little about the hierarchy of the Catholic Church. And I had nothing but an empty whiskey bottle, a few books, and cassette tapes. On my way out, I pulled a papaya off my tree and put it in my backpack.

We rode north for two hours, through the Kakamega Forest and villages even smaller than mine. When the afternoon rains came, we stopped at a duka in Webuye to buy an orange Fanta and a Cadbury chocolate bar. Paul spoke in Luhya to a few children, who wanted to touch my hair. He said they described it as tall instead of long.

After another hour of increasing elevation and decreasing temperatures, we arrived at the rectory in time for what was referred to by Paul as "spiritual hour."

"Evening prayer?" I asked.

"No," he answered. "Happy hour."

Built in the British Colonial style, Paul's home was a single-story ranch house with a metal roof, surrounded by iron gates. Someone took meticulous care of the gardens, full of thorny rosebushes in full bloom.

"Beauty is danger," Cemal had said in Tanzania. I wasn't sure if he was referring to Africa or me. But the rosebush was undoubtedly a perfect example.

Paul and I followed a houseboy down a long hallway lined with photos of all the priests who'd occupied these quarters since the turn of the century. There were pictures of dignitaries too, including former American president Jimmy Carter. We walked on a deep-blue Persian rug that looked as well worn as the house.

The hallway opened up into an expansive library, made almost entirely out of teak. Every inch of the paneled walls was covered—by bookshelves, landscape paintings, images of Jesus Christ, and taxidermy. A metal fan turned slowly on the ceiling, pushing the heat from the fireplace across the room.

An extremely old man in priestly black robes, sitting in a red-leather chair next to the fire, stood to greet us.

"Welcome!" he said loudly. "You must be Nancy from the swimming pool."

"Yes, pleased to meet you, sir. I mean Reverend."

Paul interrupted. "He's a bishop."

"Call me John," the bishop said, extending his hand to shake mine.

John pointed toward the bottles of gin, vodka, and whiskey on the brass bar top on the other side of the room.

"Help yourself," he said. "I recommend the Jameson. Neat. Ice is for tourists."

Paul poured one for each of us. The bishop motioned that I was to sit to his right, in the matching red-leather chair. Paul took a seat on the weathered black sofa, partially covered with a sheepskin throw, directly across from us.

"We don't see many mermaids in these parts," the bishop said. "How'd you wash up on the shores of Lake Victoria?"

I told him about my Peace "Corpse" work in Maragoli. I described my decorated career as a swimmer and my search for a new identity overseas.

"Are you Catholic?" he asked.

"I'm Episcopalian. Yank rebel. Sorry."

The bishop laughed and poured himself another round from a silver flask on his side table. "I like you very much," he said. "You must come whenever you like."

He told me about his move to Kenya in 1965, the year I was born. I asked if he ever got lonely or regretted the decision to give his life over to God and come to Africa. Paul winced at my frankness. John answered without any sign of being annoyed. He liked the big questions.

"Living in rural Africa is the greatest religious experience of them all," he said. "Guy de Maupassant said that 'God is everywhere except in church,' and I'm inclined to agree with him."

"So why do you build huge expensive churches in poor villages?"

Paul tried to intervene, but the bishop held up his hand.

"It's a fair question," he said. "Because I do believe the structure itself offers sanctuary, especially here. Shelter from the storm, to quote Bob Dylan. We can't build a house for everyone, but we can build one for all to share."

"That's a good answer, sir," I said.

The houseboy returned to take me to a bedroom at the other end of the hall from where we'd entered. My quarters smelled of aging leather, perhaps from the ripped chaise lounge or the zebra-skin rug. A crystal vase with a freshly cut rose sat on the mantel.

The houseboy laid my backpack on one of the twin beds, both covered in gray wool blankets. He lit the wood in my fireplace.

"*Baridi hapa,*" he said in Swahili. *Cold here.*

"*Jina loko ni nani?*" I asked. *What is your name?*

"Peter."

The bishop most likely had given him this Christian name to replace his tribal one.

Peter pointed toward the bathroom, where a steaming tub was waiting for me. A carefully selected book, *West with the Night* by Beryl Markham, had been placed by the bath. After Peter excused himself, I soaked in lavender-scented bubbles and read the first line out loud, just as I had when reading *So Long a Letter* to my students.

> *How is it possible to bring order out of memory? I should like to begin at the beginning, patiently, like a weaver at his loom.*

Peter returned an hour later to escort me to the dining room. I gave him the papaya from my backpack. The bishop certainly didn't need it. The rectory had everything in abundance. During happy hour, we'd snacked on peanuts from Dublin and cheese from London.

Taking his seat at the end of a long table, the bishop offered a prayer and a toast. "To God and our guest," he said, clinking my crystal wineglass and then Paul's.

I was surprised to find a traditional Kenyan meal of *ugali* and *sukuma wiki*—corn meal and collard greens—inside the Limoges china serving set. Forgoing his sterling-silver flatware, the bishop used his right hand to break off a piece of ugali, using it to scoop up the sukuma wiki and sop up the green juices. He ate in the style of the Kenyans he'd been living among for decades. The three of us finished a bottle of wine and the meal quickly, without making small talk— the silence eerily reminiscent of family dinners with my dad back in Florida during my youth.

After a dish of lime sherbet, we retired to the library for nightcaps. I sat on the couch while John and Paul reviewed the service for the next morning. They spoke in Luhya. I recognized the phrase *"Nyasaye n'omulayi." God is good.*

I helped myself to seconds and thirds of sherry, as did the bishop. I indulged myself in a crush on the old man. He was safe, and I was feeling more dangerous with each sip of alcohol.

We bid our goodnights just before eleven o'clock. The bishop encouraged me to return to my quarters with a wee dram of whiskey.

"Just in case you can't sleep," he said, sauntering off with one of his own.

Paul walked me down the hall and wished me *"lala salama." A good sleep.*

"See you at breakfast," he said. "Service begins at nine a.m. The church is a short walk from here."

It felt like an awkward first date in high school had come to a close. Not entirely sure what to do, I blew Paul a kiss even though I was only a foot away from him. He turned pink and walked away.

In my room, I took off all my clothes—keeping Cemal's lion claw around my neck—and got under the smooth sheets. The weight of the wool blanket warmed and comforted me. The fire had long since gone out. I wondered where Cemal was sleeping. In his house? At our room in the Kilimanjaro? With someone else? I was in a house in the middle of nowhere, with three men who shared names with Jesus's disciples. Two of them were married to God, the other their servant.

Suddenly, someone was knocking on my door. I prayed it was Cemal, who'd sworn he'd find me again. We'd speed away from the rectory in his Land Rover and I'd convert to Islam as soon as we arrived in Dar. I'd become his first and last wife.

"Yes?" I said in my loudest whisper.

"May I come in?" Paul said softly.

"Yes."

He walked into the center of the room and stood on the zebra skin.

"Do you have everything you need?" he asked.

"Mostly."

"What can I get you?"

I wanted him to kiss me, but I wasn't about to say it. How could I tempt a man of God in this holy place? I'd already lost Cemal to Allah.

"Bless me or exorcise me or something," I said very seriously. "I'm having very dark thoughts."

Paul walked over and put his lips on mine, briefly but forcefully. I asked if he could stay. He shook his head, but lay down next to me on top of the covers anyway. He stared at the ceiling, seemingly paralyzed.

"What do you want?" I asked.

"I don't know."

"Do you want to have sex?"

"Yes, but I can't. And I haven't."

"I can do it without you."

"Go ahead," he said.

Paul sipped from my whiskey while I pleasured myself. When I was done, he abruptly sat up and left the room. I was pretty sure he'd do the same thing when he got back to his room. Maybe everyone in the rectory was masturbating on this frigid evening.

Eight hours later, I was in a church pew watching Paul at the altar giving a passionate sermon in Luhya. We were the only white people in the sanctuary, which was filled with at least two hundred Kenyans. The scene was reminiscent of the Octopus Club but with pious hymns instead of dansi music. The congregation swung their hips while belting out the lyrics. I recognized the songs from my Sunday-school days and sang along. I kept my hips quiet.

I came forward to take communion, as I had in the Episcopal church of my youth. More than peace with God, though, I wanted redemption with Paul. He placed a piece of bread in my mouth before lifting the wine chalice to my lips—a far more intimate act than our late-night encounter. The single sip of wine—the blood of Christ—brought all the residual wine in my bloodstream back into play. I felt drunk again, and blissfully so.

After the service, Paul drove me the three hours home. We stopped for sodas again, but spoke very little to each other. Our easy way with one another had evaporated. When he dropped me off at Munzatsi School that afternoon, I struggled to find the right words to say. *Thank you?*

I asked Paul to wait while I ran into my house. I grabbed my Mick Jagger cassette, titled *She's the Boss*, and handed it to him. I pointed to Mick's image on the cover.

"One of my students asked if this was a picture of me," I told him.

"I can see the resemblance," Paul laughed. His dark hair and pale skin gave him a slight resemblance to the young John Lennon.

"See you at the pool sometime?" I asked.

"Insha'Allah," he answered. *God willing.*

THE PERSIAN GULF

March 28, 2015

I pray that God is willing to give me a normal blood-pressure reading. I pray that I am fine despite my drinking. *Can you hear me, God? It's me, Nancy.*

As the nurse wraps the inflatable cuff around my arm, I feel panic begin to rise. I try to control my breathing as I did in the pools of my youth and in the waiting area moments ago.

I sense my systolic pressure register, and my diastolic seconds later. They click early, which indicates an elevated reading. The nurse shakes her head when the cuff deflates and makes a note on my chart. "I'll take it again. Seems high."

I calm myself with thoughts of swimming in the Indian Ocean with David on our recent trip to Muscat, Oman. On the flight over, I told David about my failed trip to Zanzibar in 1987. I explained how Oman was a sultanate, like Zanzibar had been. In the late seventeenth century, the imam of Oman defeated the Portuguese for rule of the spice-trade ports from Mombasa to Zanzibar. I said nothing about Cemal.

David listened intently, curious about my history in the world. Was he was trying to figure out his own place in it? We landed at eleven p.m., and I was glad to see the duty-free shop still open. I bought three bottles of wine for our two-day trip. I was likely to have a hard time finding a liquor store in Muscat, since alcohol was forbidden for Muslims in Oman, just like in the UAE.

The next day marked the high holiday of Eid al-Adha, honoring Ibrahim's willingness to sacrifice his son Isaac for God. The angel Gabriel intervened at the last moment, sparing the boy. No liquor would be for sale anywhere on the Arabian Peninsula out of respect to Allah, Ibrahim, and Isaac. But plenty of livestock would be slaughtered. Our cabdriver in Muscat, who we'd hired to take us everywhere, presented David and me with a bowl of freshly killed and cooked goat meat from his own family's feast.

Warm memories of Oman are interrupted by the sound of numbers. The nurse is talking to me.

"What did you say?" I ask.

"I said 155 over 99. It's high."

She motions for me to stand on the scale. I follow her instructions.

"Ninety-two point five kilograms."

I convert the amount into pounds on my iPhone and gasp. I weigh 204 pounds—65 more than when I'd been a swimmer. I calculate the conversion again, just to be sure. The exact number is 203.92. I want to go back to the time when 23.69 ruled my life.

LAKE VICTORIA

April 1987

My number-one enemy in Maragoli was loneliness, which grew markedly worse after Tanzania. Beer made good company, even though it was a challenge to obtain in my village, especially because traditional Kenyan women weren't supposed to drink alcohol. And because liquor was hard to come by in those parts, many men made their own cheap and toxic home brew—so strong that they'd pass out for days.

I hired my eldest male student to go to the next town over and buy a case of beer for me there. I paid for his matatu ride, and two shillings for the service. I swore the boy to secrecy even though there was no disguising the heavy, clanking delivery he made to my door, even under the cover of darkness. But according to the newspapers I read at the Sunset Hotel, a lot of Kenyans hid things from their neighbors. Abuse. Addiction. Adultery. No different from Americans.

I started inventing other reasons for students to make deliveries to my house to distract from the increasing number of beer runs. I asked one of the girls to bring a cat to help curb my house's rat population. She arrived late one night in the middle of a torrential rainstorm. When

I opened my door, she handed me a burlap sack that seemed to contain a Tasmanian devil or a whirling dervish.

"Madam, it is a cat," she said. I handed her a shilling.

When I closed my door and opened the bag, out ran an enraged black cat. He scurried up my wall and into the thatched roof, where I could hear the rats scatter. The cat ran into the hills a few days later, and I was alone again.

Sometimes the crushing loneliness even made the short walk over to my classroom seem impossible. On those days, I hid in my bed with the mosquito netting drawn, while my students sat behind their desks and waited for me in vain. No one came to check if I was sick. They didn't want to disturb me.

Whenever I showed up to teach after a short self-imposed exile, the head student would inevitably say, "Madam, you were in shortage." I simply nodded and carried on with my lesson plan.

I decided to find a project to help pass the time and landed on the notion of building a library. I enlisted my students to write letters to my friends and family back in Florida, requesting financial assistance.

Two months later, envelopes with checks started coming. I skipped school many afternoons to walk the four kilometers to the post office and back. My students understood that I was working on their behalf and would sometimes walk with me.

One day, I returned to my house to find a young Danish man waiting on the steps. In perfect English, he said his name was Hugo and that someone in Kisumu had sent him to find me.

"Who?" I asked.

"A Jesuit priest," he answered.

I laughed, welcoming Hugo inside.

Hugo had traveled overland from West Africa to East Africa with friends after graduating from high school. He'd run out of money and needed a place to stay before trekking into Nairobi for his flight back to Copenhagen. I was happy to house the handsome blond, blue-eyed young man.

Hugo stayed for two weeks—sharing the mosquito netting, water tank, beer, and my body. He played basketball and soccer with the local boys while I worked on plans for the library. Money was starting to pour in, with my father's Rotary International club agreeing to fund the bulk of the construction costs.

No one at the school questioned my relationship with Hugo. He was just the white man at the white lady's house. I think the Maragolis saw it as a kind of marriage and were relieved that I no longer lived alone. I gave Hugo the job of getting the beer. But I couldn't figure out what to do with the empty ones. Bottles piled up to the ceiling in my spare room. I wasn't sure how to get rid of them without everyone in Maragoli taking notice. Neither could Hugo.

"I think you drink too much," he said once, waking to see me with a beer in my hand lying next to him. With the saddest look in his eyes, he told me that his parents were alcoholics and that he'd come to Africa to put some distance between him and them.

I hated that my drinking upset him, but I despised his judgment even more. I wasn't a drunk, for God's sake. Beer was my reward for enduring this post in the middle of East Africa. I'd earned every drop.

"I think you should leave," I told Hugo.

And he did.

I eventually left too. Construction had begun on the library; books were arriving. I spoke with the Peace Corps officer in Kisumu and told him that I'd done my best for Munzatsi Secondary School and I didn't see how I could possibly put in another year, as per my contract.

"I'm losing my mind," I told him. Extreme alienation was a common issue among volunteers, and leaving early was an option for those who felt their sanity slipping away. I'd also lost a considerable amount of weight—with a mere 125 pounds on my five-ten frame—which worried him.

After a two-hour conversation about my bowels and angst, I was issued the equivalent of an honorable discharge. He instructed me to return with my things in a week, at which time I'd be given a plane ticket back to Florida.

My first stop after leaving his office was the Sunset Hotel, to tell Odinga that I was leaving.

"Madam, I will become very sad," he said, shaking my hand. "Who will bring you the beer where you are going?"

I put a ten-shilling note in his breast pocket.

"Don't worry about me, Odinga."

I returned to my school and gathered the students. We sat on the same boulder where I'd read *So Long a Letter* and I told them I was going back to the United States.

"You'll have the library, and I expect you to read to yourselves after it's complete and full of books. Come here to this rock, and let your mind travel to many places."

They hung their heads in unison, showing their collective sadness but also their willingness to comply with my instructions.

"And you must write to me. I'll leave my address with the headmaster."

I hardly ever saw the headmaster, because he lived far away and only popped in to the school for occasional visits. But I'd been able to tell him that I was leaving before I told the students. And he didn't seem surprised.

"You need to be with your own people," he said.

"I don't know where they are," I told him. "But I'm going to try to find them."

And when I do, I told myself, *we're going to celebrate.*

THE PERSIAN GULF

March 28, 2015

The scales and the blood-pressure reading say I'm overweight and hypertensive. So what I say is just add them to my ever-growing list of screwed-up identities: washed-up swimmer; chronic drunk; dried-out nymph.

The nurse at Burjeel takes me into an examining room, where a female Indian doctor is sitting behind a large metal desk. The framed diploma on her wall shows that she's earned a medical degree from a university in England. My father would approve, so I do.

"Good morning," she says. "How can I help you today?"

"I need a refill of Celexa, an antidepressant prescription from America. I think it's also called citalopram. I've run out."

I push my empty bottle toward her.

The doctor's perfectly tweezed eyebrows furrow.

"Internists here can only prescribe a small amount of these kinds of medicines. I need to make a call to be sure."

She picks up the phone to dial the pharmacist. She asks for clarity regarding the regulation of antidepressants in the UAE. I can only hear her side of the conversation, and it's distressing.

"Hmm. Ah. Yes, I understand. How long? Then what? I see."

I put my hand on my forehead. Will I get the medicine? Should I quit drinking? Do I even want to? I've long since convinced myself that life without a hangover would be too easy. With one, I had something to overcome every single day—a guaranteed victory.

After my sophomore year of college, I asked my father if I could quit swimming. We were eating at our favorite lunch spot. I told him that I was tired of the pool after fifteen years of constant training and racing. I wanted to be liberated from the monotony. I wanted a new identity, a reason to live besides racing against time. I wanted to go somewhere other than the end of a pool and back.

"No," he said. That was all. No explanation. No negotiation.

Instead of feeling sorry for myself and angry with him, I vowed to swim harder and faster than ever. I'd become so strong and so fast that nothing and no one could hurt me. I'd make the Olympic cut in the process. My only sources of comfort on Earth were records, ribbons, medals, and trophies. They never let me down.

While my doctor continues speaking with the pharmacist, I close my eyes and remember where I was when I said one final good-bye to swimming. A time and place where I lost hope, as well as myself.

THE HAN RIVER

December 21, 1988

Post-Kenya, I spent four months at my mom's house in Florida trying to find work in South Korea.

"Why there?" she'd asked.

"The Olympics will be in Seoul in seven months. I have to be there!"

"Why don't you just go for the Games and get a job here in Florida?"

"Mom, have you met me?"

We both laughed, knowing that once I had an idea in my head, I couldn't let it go. My former rival Angel was set to compete in the 50-meter freestyle at the 1988 Summer Olympic Games after breaking the American record in the event. If Angel won the gold medal in Seoul, I wanted to be in the stands to witness it. I'd beaten her in a handful of races before losing to her in the last one.

The Peace Corps mailed biweekly job listings, with details of other overseas employment options, to former volunteers. Having served in the Peace Corps meant that you'd already withstood difficult situations in far-flung places. International organizations, especially those in Africa and Asia, were eager to get their hands on people like us.

One of the mailings mentioned a private language company with schools around the world, including in South Korea. They were looking to hire Americans to teach conversational English to businesspeople, diplomats, and graduate students. The pay was excellent. Flights and housing were covered. I called the number of the main office in Los Angeles and got a phone interview the next day. A month later, I was on a plane bound for the Hermit Kingdom, as the Korean Peninsula was once known. The Olympics would soon bust South Korea's doors wide open, and the country needed help unlocking its potential.

Twenty-four other Americans, mostly former Peace Corps volunteers, were also employed by English Language International in the suburb of Gangnam—an up-and-coming neighborhood south of the Han River. We explored the city in packs, like wolves, and spent most nights in the red-light district alongside soldiers on leave from their posts at the Demilitarized Zone at the thirty-eighth parallel. My drinking and dancing stamina impressed my colleagues and even a few of the GIs. I could hang out in bars until two a.m. and still be in front of a class at eight a.m.

Partying helped pass the time between my arrival in April and the start of the Games in September. So did Jack, an American editor with the *Korea Herald* newspaper who I first met at the Heavy Metal Club. He'd been sipping a beer and watching me dance. I walked over to him when the Billy Idol song ended.

"What's your name?" I asked the dark-haired young man wearing an "I Love Paris" T-shirt.

"Jack."

"Wanna dance?"

"Nope."

I walked away, determined to make Jack regret turning me down. I asked the DJ to play a song by Prince and proceeded to dance as wildly as I had done at the Octopus Club.

I glanced at Jack afterward, and he was expressionless. But two days later, I found him sitting in the staff room at my school and reading a book with the cover torn off.

"What are you doing here?" I said, coming through the doors after my last evening class.

"I used to work here," he said. "I still come by to get my mail."

"And me. You came by to get me too."

He laughed. I'd broken him.

"What's with the book with no cover?"

"I don't want anyone to know what I'm reading."

"So what are you reading?"

"*Ulysses*. What are you reading?"

"*Oedipus*," I said. "You've met your match."

◆ ◆ ◆

Jack walked me home that night and every night thereafter until we moved in together a month later. He introduced me to the *Herald*'s sports editor, who was impressed by my swimming background and degree in English. He hired me on the spot to cover swimming and diving for the newspaper during the Games.

My preview of the events, which ran two weeks before the opening ceremonies, included the news that Angel had tested positive for a banned substance right after the trials and wouldn't be swimming in Seoul. Writing the piece, I couldn't help but think that I'd triumphed over my rival in the end. I'd made it to the Games and she hadn't.

I was in Jamsil Natatorium when Kristin Otto of East Germany took the gold in the 50-meter freestyle. Jill Sterkel from the United States tied for the bronze, and American Leigh Ann Fetter was fifth—all of their times significantly faster than my 23.69, which was recorded in yards, not meters.

Yet each of my bylined articles in the *Herald* felt like a gold medal. And I celebrated them with pint after pint of beer. I maintained the pace long after the Olympics had come and gone.

By winter, I felt defeated. I had no time, date, or place to obsess over, as I'd done with making the cut for the Olympic Trials and, later, coming to the Games. I began to fixate on the times and places where I could drink. Counting down the hours at school to the moment when I could lift a beer to my lips.

Jack and I continued to frequent the same clubs—he sipped a few beers while I drank four or five and danced the calories off so I could drink more. He never danced with me, just watched and wrote in his notebook. I often felt lonely in his company. Jack was quiet and brooding. He was the opposite of Cemal—the opposite of me. Earning Jack's affections and attention was hard work. And I wanted the job.

The bitterly cold wind that roared through Seoul in the late fall felt how I imagined base camp at Everest might. The decreasing hours of daylight in early winter also left me in a dark mood. I mourned the warming effect Africa had had on me, inside and out.

On a snowy morning in late December, the staff room was buzzing with talk of the two-week Christmas break. Many of my colleagues had tickets for beaches in Southeast Asia where they'd hook up with friends from other parts of the world. I'd planned to stay in Seoul, with Jack, to save money for a trip in the spring. We'd talked about going to the Philippines, where I'd been born twenty-two years earlier.

"Anyone seen Carolyn?" asked Jane, who was our head teacher with the thankless job of trying to keep track of us. She had to repeat her question more loudly to be heard. "Anyone seen Carolyn?"

"She's probably hungover and sleeping it off," I joked, lying down on the staff room's faded green corduroy couch, pulling an old wool blanket over my legs.

"You're the lush, Bercaw," Jane snapped. "Carolyn would have called. I just tried to call her, and she's not answering."

"She could be really sick," I said, feeling badly about having been flippant. "Appendix or something."

"I'll go check on her," Jane sighed. Her roommate, Marissa, offered to tag along and suggested they get one of the Korean maintenance men to drive them over in the school van. Most of the teachers lived in the same sprawling complex in Jamsil, near the Olympic stadium and pool. They took the subway back and forth to school. Jack and I lived near the clubs in Itaewon. I took a local bus to ELI from our neighborhood while he walked to the *Korea Herald*.

Carolyn's roommate was away in the United States, which meant that Carolyn was alone in her *apart*—the term Koreans used for the English word "apartments." If she were sick, no one would be on hand to help. I was glad Jane and Marissa were headed to see her and had a vehicle in case she needed to go to the hospital or something.

The three of them had spent the previous weekend hiking on Mount Seorak with a group of Korean students. Carolyn was always encouraging teachers to socialize with their classes to practice conversational English in real-life settings. A few old-timers on the staff thought Carolyn was crossing a line, but she was careful not to give the wrong impression or mislead anyone. She was very vocal about her fiancé, a Japanese man in Tokyo.

When Jane and Marissa headed out, I left for the nearby bathhouse to sweat out my toxins. After a long soak in the hottest water, I lay down on the heated floor in my towel, just as the Korean women did.

I awoke with a start, a half hour before evening classes began. I dressed quickly, gathered my things, and took a look at my wild hair, which had dried while I was asleep. I didn't have time to fix it or even brush it. I ran the short distance in the cold night air to ELI along Teheran-Ro—a road inexplicably, at least to me, named for the capital of Iran. I stormed into the staff room with five minutes to spare. A messy handwritten message on the chalkboard was waiting for me.

Emergency Staff Meeting at 5:55 p.m.

I stood staring at the words in disbelief, alongside my equally apoplectic colleagues. All of us as flummoxed by the sight of English as our beginner students. What did the sentence mean? We'd never once had a meeting. Maybe it was code. Was North Korea poised to invade?

Before anyone could venture an answer, the school's director walked into the room. A retired military officer, Tim was typically poised and commanding. He gallivanted around town with a Korean girlfriend named So Young, who was half his age. They were the source of endless jokes in the staff room. But standing before us on December 21, Tim was hunched over and grim faced, looking every one of his sixtysomething years.

"Jane and Marissa went to check on Carolyn today after she didn't show up for the morning session," he said. "I am very, very sorry."

He paused for moment, and I wondered if he was sick. Maybe everyone was coming down with the flu. What was he sorry about?

"Carolyn is dead."

He paused again.

"Jane and Marissa found her body."

Tim retrieved a handkerchief from his pocket and patted at his forehead.

"She was murdered," Tim continued. "The police are still there investigating. The embassy has informed Carolyn's family. Her father is coming to Korea to take her body back to the United States. I just spoke with him. He is distraught, as you can imagine."

I grabbed the hand of my friend Kimberly, who was standing next to me. I needed to touch someone—the way I do when I've had too much to drink. Someone to steady me, to save me.

"We'll find out who did this," Tim said. "I swear to you. We will do everything."

I couldn't process anything he was saying. Why would anyone kill Carolyn? She was as delightful as she was beautiful, not vain or mean in the slightest. She brought sunlight into our staff room when Seoul plunged into winter. Everyone, Korean and expat, had been drawn to her glow. How could it have been extinguished?

"Jane and Marissa are in a state of shock," Tim continued. "They need our support. They are still with the police, answering questions. Some of Carolyn's things were missing. Her house was ransacked."

"Are we . . . in danger?" Kimberly asked haltingly, as if she were testing the words.

"The police believe not. But that's all I know," Tim answered.

Someone tearfully asked how we could help.

"Go teach," Tim said apologetically. "This will be on the TV news tonight. Let's shelter our students for as long as we can. I know this is a shock. I honestly don't know what else to do."

I offered to take Carolyn's class in with mine, even though I had no idea what I'd say or do with them. I wanted to be sheltered too. I wanted to *unhear* everything Tim had said. I wanted to rewind to Friday afternoon, just three days earlier, when Carolyn and I had been joking around in the staff room.

"The Korean Peninsula looks like a penis," I said. "Dangling off Siberia."

"A flaccid one," Carolyn pointed out.

We fell back laughing on the big couch. Jane came out of the staff kitchen.

"What's so funny?" she asked.

Neither Carolyn nor I could answer in the midst of our hysterics. Jane rolled her eyes and went back to making tea.

Opening the door now to Carolyn's classroom, I was hit with traces of pepper spray, and a coughing fit came over me. Some of her college-age students, like mine, spent afternoons in the anti-American protests downtown. They came for night classes at ELI with tear-gas masks in their bags and Mace on their clothing. But none of us—Korean students or American teachers—ever said a word about it. So much unspoken at our language school.

The riots had increased and intensified after the Olympics. Many Koreans wanted no part of what the West had to offer, after witnessing what they called our "barbarian" ways during the Games. They hoped to push the American military presence out of their country altogether and for the two Koreas to reunite. When I'd lamented the hostility of the situation, Jack had found a way to put it in context.

"Imagine a Korean military base in the middle of Manhattan," he said. "Imagine it there for five decades, hogging prime real estate as well as the whole conversation about who really runs the place."

The tear gas from Carolyn's classroom made my eyes water profusely—but I was grateful for an excuse to tear up openly. I imagined her family back in the US and their collective outpouring of grief. How had this happened? Who could have killed Carolyn? She was the very picture of life—her blue eyes danced with delight whenever she had an idea for the classroom. She'd hosted the best Halloween party I'd ever attended, just two months earlier. Everyone she knew, including Korean students, had come in costume.

By teaching Carolyn's class, I was protecting her in a way. Her students would have a few more hours blissfully unaware of her death. I invited her class to join mine in the room next door and I let the two groups face off in a game of hangman on the chalkboard. They took turns guessing letters and filling in the blank spaces. I looked for hidden meanings in their word choices—*hello, happy, goodbye*—for signs that a murderer might be among us. But Carolyn and the rest of us had only ever taught words to live by.

◆ ◆ ◆

On Christmas Day, I went to the staff room to escape the grim reality that Carolyn had been murdered a mere four days earlier. I wanted a safe space, away from the city's climate and citizenry, in which to read. Jack had given me William Boyd's book *A Good Man in Africa* as a gift, leaving the cover intact. I'd given him *Love in the Time of Cholera* by Gabriel García Márquez.

ELI was closed for the holidays, and no doubt would have shut down for a while anyway after Carolyn's death. Few students had come to class the day after the Korean news stations showed her bloodstained bed and teddy bear. Her murder traumatized an already-polarized city.

Koreans were certain a bloodthirsty Yank had killed Carolyn. Americans, including me, were sure the murderer was a vengeful *Hanguk*, a Korean person, who probably wanted the American *Meguk* off their long-suffering peninsula for good.

With the help of a translator, the Korean cops interrogated every single ELI teacher, including me, the day after Jane and Marissa found Carolyn's body. They asked the same questions, with the same hostile tone, in one of our classrooms.

Where were you on Monday night? Were you with other people? If so, who? Give us their names and phone numbers. How well did you know the victim? Was she having a secret love affair with someone on the staff? Did any of the teachers resent her?

I couldn't understand why they were asking about the staff. We all loved Carolyn. The culprit had to be someone from outside ELI's walls. The Korean police had little experience with violent crime, it seemed, because so few happened in their country. They seemed to be playing roles from an American movie, smoking cigarettes while interviewing us—the only things missing from the scene were a dangling lightbulb over our heads and some piped-in fog. Nothing seemed real.

THE PERSIAN GULF

March 28, 2015

My doctor at Burjeel Hospital is typing something on her keyboard while continuing to converse with the pharmacist on the phone. I feel like I'm in a scene from a daytime television soap opera, but it's all too real.

"Looking that up," she says into the receiver, which is cocked between her ear and shoulder.

A lot of information pops up on her screen, but I can't make it out from where I sit. My eyesight is diminished, no doubt, by age and lifestyle. I read recently, with the help of my bifocals, that prolonged use of antimalarial medication takes a toll on vision. So does alcohol, but few people, especially not me, are willing to blame booze for their troubles, even though alcohol abuse results in the death of 88,000 Americans every year. Being murdered, like Carolyn, is rare. Yet being killed is at the top of mankind's worries.

I've long been aware of the dangers of drinking too much. Not only am I the daughter of a doctor who was obsessed with healthy living, but I'm also the granddaughter of an alcoholic who didn't live long enough to meet me.

My mom's own mother succumbed to liver cirrhosis at the age of forty-two—on the exact day I was born. Newly postpartum, my mom couldn't travel from the Philippines back to America for her mother's funeral. She was plunged into profound grief at what was supposed to be the happiest time in her life. I don't know how she managed the opposing emotions on top of my father's idiosyncrasies. Apparently he stormed around Clark Air Base Hospital shouting about how the US government was botching the war effort, and signing death certificates as George Washington.

When my father died, in 2012, after six years with Alzheimer's and eleven months in a memory-care facility, I added his disease to the top of my concerns. I relegated alcohol, the most clear and present danger to my heath, to the bottom of the list.

And here I am, three years later, trying to get a refill on a medication that is all but ineffective when taken with alcohol. Yet I'm determined to get my pills no matter how long Abu Dhabi's medical system delays the process.

I got a preview of the country's medical bureaucracy not too long after our arrival. In addition to providing what seemed like every official piece of paper we'd been issued since birth, Allan and I had to take a leprosy test and have blood drawn to check for HIV, hepatitis, and syphilis.

"Why leprosy?" I asked the nurse at the Health Screening Centre. "Isn't it almost eradicated, like polio?"

She didn't answer, which led me to believe the concern was most likely directed at the migrant laborers from India, many of whom were waiting in line behind me.

The doctor at Burjeel holds up a finger to indicate that only a moment or two remains before we'll have an answer. If I don't walk out of here with my refill, I'll be looking at a flight back to the United States as soon as possible just to get my medication. At least there's free booze on international flights.

THE HAN RIVER

December 25, 1988

While I hid in ELI's staff lounge on Christmas Day, Tim was at his desk on the first floor, buried in paperwork. He'd barely even looked up when I came in the building. I'd given him a sad little wave and a halfhearted smile as I passed by his glass window in the lobby.

Some of the teachers who hadn't left the country on vacation were holed up in their aparts. And all of those were asking for armed guards. Tim was making the arrangements.

I poured myself a beer from the staff fridge, pausing to look at the postcards stuck with magnets to the door. One was from Carolyn, who'd gone on a weekend jaunt to Jeju Island with Jane back in early November.

> *Hi guys! This place rocks. Literally. Get your asses down here to check it out. Anyohaseyo from the haenyeo!*
> *—Love, Carolyn*

Anyohaseyo was the phrase Koreans used to meet, greet, and part ways. The image on the front showed a *haenyeo*—one of the famed female deep-sea divers at the southernmost tip of Korea. She was holding an octopus over her head and smiling. She'd retrieved it from the bottom without the aid of oxygen or traps. The haenyeo women were legendary for catching fish with their bare hands in the cold, deep water.

The staff phone rang, startling me. I ran into the lounge to answer it.

"Hello?" I said. *"Yeoboseyo?"*

No response.

"Hello? Who's calling?" I asked again. I could hear shallow breathing.

"I know who killed Carolyn," whispered a timid female voice with a slight Korean accent.

"What did you say?" I was sure that I'd misheard.

"I know who killed Carolyn," she said again.

I tried to place her voice—Korean accent, excellent command of English. Not like any students at ELI. More like a Korean who had moved to the United States and returned to Seoul.

"What's your name?" I asked in the safest and calmest tone I could muster. I needed to keep her on the line.

"I know who killed Carolyn," she repeated.

"Then please tell me," I said.

"I can't."

"I think you want to. It would help a lot of people to have this information. Please help us. Please."

"I don't know if I should."

"You should," I coaxed, trying not to sound desperate. "We need you."

"An American military man whose last name begins with *P*," she blurted out before hanging up.

I ran downstairs to get Tim, who called the chief Korean investigator.

The police arrived quickly, and I repeated the phone conversation to them. Their questions confused me. I wondered if the interpreter was making mistakes in translation.

"Are you sure it was a Korean accent?"

"Yes."

"Could it have been Japanese?"

"No."

"Or an American pretending to be Korean?"

"I can't be sure of that."

"Are you sure it was a female voice?"

"Yes."

"Had you ever heard it before?"

"I don't think so."

Their questions seemed to be implying something that I couldn't quite decipher. They most certainly didn't trust my assessment of the caller, and tried to sway me away from the idea that she had been a Korean.

When the police left after about an hour, Tim came upstairs to tell me that an Army Criminal Investigation Command agent was on his way. The American military was getting involved in the case because the phone call had implicated a US soldier.

"Thank God," I said.

Tim, himself a former army officer, looked relieved as well. At the very least, we'd get to speak with someone for whom English was the first language. So much seemed to be getting lost in translation.

When the special agent arrived, he asked me to repeat every single word of the phone call. He seemed familiar with the case. And his questions seemed in line with the situation as I perceived it.

"Do you think the caller was a student here?" he asked.

"Her English was better than most of our students. Her verb tense was exact. And she didn't roll her *L*s into *R*s. She'd probably spent time in the United States. A Korean American. But back in Seoul for long enough to revert to old accents."

"Did you hear any background noise? Did it sound long-distance or local? Clear line or a delay?"

"I was really focusing on getting her to say who killed Carolyn. The whole thing was so weird. I didn't have time to think."

"Did Carolyn know any military men?" he asked.

"I didn't socialize that much with her, except for parties at the teachers' aparts. Sometimes random GIs showed up. We dance with military guys in Itaewon, but none of us go for their type. Besides, they all want to screw Korean girls. Sorry, I didn't mean to say that."

"Do you think Carolyn might have been involved with one?"

"I really don't think so," I answered. "She had a fiancé. Japanese. She really loved the guy. He was supposed to come the day before Christmas. Oh my God, he was supposed to be here with her now, celebrating Christmas."

The agent said that he'd file his report to get a full-blown investigation under way—an entirely separate entity from the Korean one. The army had already been waiting for a reason to get involved. Carolyn's father was working on getting the FBI involved too.

I took the subway from Gangnam Station to Jane and Marissa's apart in Jamsil. I was eager to share the news of a potential break in the case. I knew they'd be relieved. I was so happy to be the bearer of good news after all they'd been through.

"Help is on the way!" I said with all the enthusiasm I could muster, walking inside their half-open door. We were under strict orders to lock ourselves inside our aparts, even if we were only home for a minute or two. "Ladies, be sure the door is closed and locked!"

"The Korean police just left," Jane said. "They had more questions."

Jane and Marissa were sitting at their dining-room table with an uneaten pizza in front of them. Both had withered in the four days since they'd found Carolyn's lifeless body.

"You'll be able to eat when you hear this," I said and proceeded to tell them everything about the phone call and the CID officer assigned to the case.

"You are so naive, Nancy," Jane lashed out at me. "You think this CID guy is going to solve the case just because he's an American?"

"Jane, I thought you'd be happy to hear this news. At least we can talk to someone, in English, about what happened. And he can answer us in English. It's an improvement, if not a solution."

Marissa got up and tossed the entire pizza in the trash. She gagged, almost throwing up.

"We can't turn against each other when this whole country is out to get us," I said. "I'll make us some tea; let's try to stay calm."

Jane nodded sadly. She went over to her couch to watch the snow falling lightly outside the window. She seemed half-dead, like a prisoner of war.

I looked around the kitchen for supplies. I found a few tea bags in a container, a few slices of bread and some jelly in the otherwise-empty fridge. Locating a knife proved more difficult. I looked through every drawer and in the dishwasher. Nothing but forks and spoons everywhere I searched.

I don't know why—maybe because I'm tall and they were low—I haphazardly stuck my right hand on top of the kitchen cupboards. I felt around frantically, bumping into something that clanked. I stood on a chair to see what I'd hit.

Every single cutting tool in the house was on top of the cupboard. Steak knives, bread knives, chopping knives, even butter knives. Why had my friends put them there? Did they fear they were the next targets?

My stomach cramped and I stepped down. I made a mental note to hide my knives too. Doing so seemed like a good idea if a killer was on the loose. I was glad I lived with Jack, who worked out every day and had a fierce expression. Koreans seemed intimidated by him.

I walked into Jane and Marissa's living room with two teacups. Marissa was asleep in a chair. Jane was writing a letter on the coffee table. I put a cup down in front of her and kept the other for myself.

"Who to?" I asked softly.

"To whom?" Jane corrected me, suppressing a giggle. I was happy to give her something to laugh at.

"Carolyn's eldest sister. You can read it."

The letter began with Jane's explanation of how she'd become friends with Carolyn. Upon their introduction, Carolyn had mentioned that Jane resembled her eldest sister. Jane then explained how Carolyn was always the life of the staff room—dancing and singing—and had inspired Jane to experience more with her students out of the classroom.

Jane went on to say that she and Marissa had been the ones who'd found Carolyn, and how difficult things had been since. She also said just how much Carolyn was adored and respected, and that she was an exceptional teacher and friend.

She ended the letter by offering to help Carolyn's family in any way.

"Well done," I said, putting my hand on her back. "I'm sure it will comfort her family to know Carolyn was beloved here. By you, and all of us."

"Thanks, Nancy," Jane responded. "Maybe we should have a memorial service in the staff room. I could give a eulogy."

"That's a great idea. I'll organize the food. Let's do it on the first day back after the New Year. I'll call the others when I get home. You get some rest."

I went back to the apart I shared with Jack to relay the news of the day. We drank the six-pack of Bud Light I'd bought at the USO after our trip to the DMZ on Thanksgiving Day. Facing North Korea, on the military demarcation line, I never could have imagined that my life would be bisected here too.

Jack had spent the morning sniffing around the *Korea Herald*'s newsroom for any information he could get about Carolyn's case. But even though the paper's reporters wrote in English, they spoke with each other in Korean. And unlike in American investigations, Korean police didn't share information with the media.

One *Herald* journalist had managed to get a quote from an unidentified cop: "We suspect the murder was a crime of passion or a personal grudge in view of its savagery."

But the *Chosun Ilbo*, a Korean daily paper, was reporting the opposite: "Police, reversing earlier statements, said it now appeared a number of items, including a camera and a tape recorder, had been removed from the apartment and there were signs of ransacking."

Jack and I reviewed every detail over and over again, looking for a mistake, a break, a gap, a clue, or a motive. Had it been a crime of passion or botched burglary?

When the beer ran out, I suggested we hit the *soju* tent at the end of our street. I didn't love the clear Korean alcohol as much as I liked vodka, but it was my only option at that late hour.

My need to be inebriated had escalated in the days since Carolyn's death. And at 20 percent alcohol by volume, soju was potent enough to wipe thoughts of her dead body out of my head. I'd seen the haunting news video of her being carried out of her apartment on a stretcher, a sheet over her remains. The first few sips of booze made the mental picture fray at its edges; drinking the whole bottle sent the image up in flames.

Jack and I took seats at one of the tables near a kerosene heater and a tightly sealed section of the thick canvas tent, to protect us from Seoul's bitter wind. A handful of blurry-eyed Korean businessmen in black coats looked up at us from their drinks and peanuts.

"*Soju dugay juseyo,*" I told the server. *Two sojus, please.*

He retrieved the small bottles and put them in front of us with two tiny cups.

"*Anju?*" I asked, indicating that we'd like snacks as well.

The server grabbed a small octopus from the fish tank on his work-space and proceeded to hack off its legs. He put the squirming append-ages on a plate for Jack and me to share.

"*Ani!*" I said, pushing the plate back toward him. *No!*

Jack squeezed my arm. "Don't be rude, Nancy," he said. "We should eat it, out of respect."

"Respect for whom? The Koreans or the octopus?"

"Both." He pulled the plate back and thanked our server. "*Kamsamnida.*"

I'd sworn to never consume *nakji*. I didn't like the brutal way in which the octopus was slaughtered, and I didn't like the fact that swal-lowing live arms could choke me. But that was part of the dish's allure—a game of who'd kill the other first.

Jack picked up his chopsticks and tried to trap an arm that seemed to be fighting back. He finally stabbed it, shoving the thing in his mouth and washing it down with a shot of soju.

The businessman sitting to the left of Jack patted his back. "*Nay,*" he said, pointing to me. *Yes.*

Korean men believed eating living octopus increased their sexual stamina. Jack didn't need added stamina, because I liked to fuck fast and furiously. I didn't see the value in endless humping. If the point was to climax, then get to the finish line.

"Let's leave this place, Jack. Make our way to Kenya after the Philippines. I'll take you to the Octopus Club. We'll swim in the Indian Ocean in Mombasa," I suggested. "Imagine walking on the beach in the warm sun. Thousands of miles from here. All of this behind us."

Jack nodded. He'd been in Seoul for two years and was ready to move on. We finished the soju and ordered more, toasting to our impending departure from the Hermit Kingdom. A fresh batch of octo-pus was delivered with the bottle. I grabbed a wriggling arm with my hands and shoved it in my mouth. I tried to swallow it, but it came right up again—the severed limb dangled from my lips.

THE PERSIAN GULF

March 28, 2015

The doctor hangs up the phone and stares at my bloodshot eyes.

"Allergies," I mutter, trying to blame Abu Dhabi's climate for their appearance. "What did the pharmacist say?"

"I can give you a thirty-day refill of the medicine. After that you have to see a specialist for a full psychiatric evaluation to get any more."

Our family has sixty days left in Abu Dhabi before heading back to Vermont. I could cut each pill in half to stretch the medication out. I've done it before, and can do it again, with few noticeable side effects.

But the greatest challenge still lies before me—getting out of Burjeel Hospital without mention of my general health.

The doctor begins filling out my prescription. *Homestretch.* She pauses to look over my chart. *Nearing the finish line.*

"How do you pronounce your last name?" she asks.

Relieved she isn't inquiring about my blood-pressure reading, I answer flippantly. "In Kenya, it was Bird-Cow. Americans often mistake it for Bearclaw. In Korea, I thought of myself as Brr-caw."

My dad used to say "Pride cometh before a fall" whenever I got cocky about my swimming. And by the expression overtaking my doctor's face, I was about to hit rock bottom.

"Ms. Bercaw," she says, pronouncing my name perfectly, "I see that your blood pressure is very high. Do you take any medication for this condition?"

Crap. Fuck. Shit.

"Um, no, I'm nervous. You know, white-coat syndrome. I see a doctor and my blood pressure goes up."

"What was your last reading? When was your last physical exam?"

"Before we moved to Abu Dhabi last August," I lie. "Eight months ago."

I'd actually avoided my hometown doctor ever since she'd declared my liver to be swollen in 2013 and sent me for an ultrasound. The results showed fatty-liver disease. I saw a specialist, who told me to limit processed foods and abstain from alcohol until it resolved. He called it "adrenal fatigue." I'd been relieved not to hear the word *alcoholism* and I most certainly hadn't given him any reason to say it.

By the intense expression on my Burjeel doctor's face, I can tell she wants to get to the root cause of my problems.

"We need to understand why your blood pressure is elevated and treat the cause," she details. "I'd like to schedule you for lab work, then a follow-up appointment."

She hands me the prescription for my medication and a slip for the pathology lab on the main floor. "Get the blood drawn now," she says. "And come back in three days so we can start to figure this out before something happens to you."

"Thank you, Doctor." I nod respectfully, as if I were in Korea.

I walk to the reception desk, pay my bill, and make a follow-up appointment with no intention of keeping it. I thank my fellow Filipina for her help and leave through the main door. I take the elevator to the ground floor and walk right past Pathology on my way to the pharmacy.

THE INDIAN OCEAN

May 1, 1989

Jack and I arrived in Mombasa after random and extended stopovers in Manila, Bangkok, Hong Kong, Beijing, Kathmandu, and New Delhi—a route selected entirely by the cheapest flights available from each location. Back in Kenya, the last thing I wanted to think about was Korea, but a thin blue airmail envelope, postmarked from Seoul, was waiting for me at the post office. And even though it was from my pal Kimberly, I was reluctant to open it.

Still, I was curious for news on everyone. How was Jane managing? With our encouragement, she'd gone back to the States to recover shortly after Carolyn's memorial service. I wondered if the school had recuperated from the negative press. Were there any leads on Carolyn's killer? When I'd left Seoul in February, every investigator, including the army's special agent, was coming up empty. Jack and I figured the case would remain as cold as Seoul.

Traveling from country to country, drinking beer after beer, I managed to distance myself physically and emotionally from the tragedy. But the mere sight of Kimberly's handwriting brought my buried grief to the surface. My stomach churned. I sat down on the bed in the Arab guesthouse with the unopened letter in my hand and a Tusker beer on the side table.

Carolyn's memorial service popped into my head. Jane had led a moving and tearful tribute to her fallen friend. Marissa had made a shrine with candles around a picture of Carolyn, and we all toasted with whiskey to her truth and beauty. On the same blackboard that had once announced *Emergency Meeting at 5:55*, someone had written the words *Contrary to what Voltaire said, this is not the best of all possible worlds.*

Later, over pitchers of beer at the Nashville Club in Itaewon, Jane announced that she'd be returning to her home in Montana the next day. Distraught and skeletal, she'd lost at least fifteen pounds off her already-slender frame. We supported her decision, with enthusiasm. Jane needed time and space to heal from what she'd seen and endured.

Marissa needed reprieve as well, but she wanted to stick it out in Seoul until summer. She was close to earning a bonus for two full years at ELI, which she planned to use for bankrolling graduate school.

Kimberly decided to stay on too, at least until one of her job applications elsewhere came through. I told the group that Jack and I were leaving in February to head in the direction of Africa. They'd be able to write me care of the Mombasa post office.

Five months later, I was holding a letter from Kimberly in my tanned hands on the Swahili coast. I took a huge gulp of Tusker beer and opened it.

> *Dear Nancy,*
> *Thank you for the colorful postcard! It helped me for-*
> *get that from my desk (yes, desk!), I am staring at the*
> *Mokhwa Wedding Hall and unconsciously observing doz-*
> *ens of hope-filled Korean girls enter marital hell.*
>
> *Meanwhile, I'm happy to report that I have a mere*
> *45 days left in the Land of the Morning Calm. I have a*

plane ticket, a room, and a job waiting in Taipei. I look forward to hot-hot weather, bad beer, and taking life as un-seriously as I can. I believe that will be the best remedy for the hostility which has been awakened in me here. As for ELI—lots of new faces (and they're getting stranger all the time, I sincerely believe that some of these creatures could benefit from a neurological consultation with your father). This month (that is, next week), Ginger is off (to ELI Madrid) and Doris is off to Nepal (USIS school in Kathmandu). Both are happily contemplating departure. It's pathetic how happy we all become before we leave, isn't it?

Now for the hard part. I feel like I've been writing a circle around this—and since I don't know who you are in touch with, I don't know how much you know. If this is all news to you, then I'm very sorry that you have to hear it from me.

Apparently, Jane Peterson may have killed Carolyn in a fit of unreturned love, and Marissa returned to the scene to help try to cover it up by disguising it as a robbery. All this came out when Marissa failed the polygraph test she was forced to take before she suddenly decided to head back to the States too.

Well, as you may know, Marissa is still here, not in custody but unable to leave the country. Apparently, Jane can't be extradited because the US & Korea don't have an extradition agreement. The second-scariest thing is that it looks like they're going to get away with it. The scariest thing is the US gov't investigators have uncovered an identical unsolved crime, which occurred in Thailand while Jane was there. No doubt a coincidence . . .

Meanwhile, Jane was writing chummy notes to her friends here even after we'd all found out. Then Carolyn's father got in contact with Jane (over the phone) and went nuts. Then Jane called Tim and insisted that she hadn't done it.

So. So. So. Now it's over and nobody knows exactly what's going on. So many new people have washed in that it's no longer a current issue. Marissa's out of sight, living in a yogwan downtown, I believe, unable to understand why people were so shocked, hurt, and angry when this all came out. I know it seems unbelievable—we were all in shock for two weeks after—but then you reach a saturation point or something. I don't know. I look at my photos from Korea, and Jane & Marissa are in at least half of them since we took all our holidays together, and I just shake my head.

Well, best wishes to you & Jack both. I'll send you my address from Taipei.

Love,

K

I couldn't move a muscle. I couldn't speak, let alone scream. I put the letter on my stomach, trying to absorb the contents by physical contact. Kimberly's words were inconceivable, but also made perfect sense. I replayed the circumstances surrounding Carolyn's death.

Jane and Marissa going to "find out" if Carolyn was okay when she didn't show up for work—and taking a maintenance man with them. Establishing a witness to their "discovery" of Carolyn's body was a stroke of Machiavellian genius. I drank the rest of my beer in one swallow.

The phone call I'd received in the staff room implicating a military man whose last name began with P. Had Jane, last name Peterson, set up someone to make that call? Maybe she'd taken a page from some

Psychopath's Handbook that had suggested giving a tiny clue about your identity while sending others on a wild-goose chase. Jane knew I was headed to the staff room for solace on Christmas Day. Maybe the voice on the line actually belonged to Marissa, who was a linguist with a knack for accents. Jane was convincing, clever, and calculating. She'd moved everyone around like chess pieces. Except the Korean police, who had probably been on to her from the very start. Hence, their indefatigable interest in the same line of questioning every time.

Sitting with them at their apartment after the phone call. Had I been comforting the alleged criminals all along? "Whoever killed Carolyn also destroyed me," Jane had said when I served her tea. I recalled the dance party we'd had at Jane and Marissa's apartment when Carolyn first came to Seoul. Jane played "Psycho Killer" by Talking Heads over and over again while everyone danced wildly. We all loved the song, but she seemed particularly devoted to it. And then she'd fixated on "Fast Car" by Tracy Chapman after Carolyn's death.

The knives above their cupboard? Had the murder weapon been among them? Why hadn't I questioned my bizarre findings? I'd been so eager to explain the knives' hiding place as a safety precaution. In fact, everything Jane and Marissa had done after Carolyn's death was a legitimate response to what they'd been through. I never once considered their behavior as the manifestation of two people trying to suppress a crime. Jane had called me naive. Had I proved her right by getting the whole knife thing wrong?

Jane's eulogy for Carolyn. A brilliant strategy—maybe from a subsequent chapter in a little-known guide to covering psychopathic tracks: Play the role of angst-ridden friend to the zenith. And while you're at it, write to her family and offer your sympathies. Tell them how much she meant to you. Oh, and then announce in front of everyone that you have to leave Seoul for your own mental health. The very people you might have manipulated will support your decision. *Yes, go! We love you! You need to save yourself from these horrible Koreans!*

Now Jane was on the other side of the world, with no extradition agreement to force her to return to Seoul to stand trial for what she'd been accused of doing by Marissa. Had she gotten away with murder?

The real question was how I'd go on with my life. How any of us from ELI would, for that matter. "Jack!" I called out. He was immersed in a book on the balcony. "Let's go swim in the ocean."

Sitting at the shoreline of the blue-green water, I listened to the noontime call to prayer coming from the nearest mosque. I let the sound of the muezzin's rich voice carry me to a safe place in my head before telling Jack about the contents of Kimberly's letter.

When I was done, I lay back on the wet sand so the incoming tide could cool my warm skin. Jack followed suit.

"Jesus," he said. "Impossible yet possible."

"Bingo!" I yelled, just as I had done in Dar, a mere five hundred kilometers to our south, three years earlier with Cemal. "So what do we do now?"

I turned my head so my eyes were level with the sand. I watched a tiny crab dash into a hole.

"Nothing," Jack said. "There's nothing that can be done. Justice is a matter of jurisdiction. Without an extradition agreement, Jane can't be sent back to South Korea for trial. She's innocent until proven guilty. Free to live her life, like us."

"But we're not free," I answered. "We're trapped by this event. Forever. Wherever we are in the world, we will be haunted by what happened to Carolyn in Seoul and the lack of resolution in the case."

I allowed my mind to wander. If Jane really had stabbed Carolyn to death, then she'd also put a metaphorical dagger in the rest of our backs. Jesus, how could she have killed her best friend and then lied to the rest of us about it? Yet it sounded like the Korean police really believed that Jane could be the culprit, and that Marissa's confession was their best piece of evidence. The possibility remained that Jane hadn't done this awful thing and that Marissa had gone off her rocker. "If Jane did it, I wish something bad would happen to her."

"Remember what Gandhi said?" Jack cautioned. "An eye for an eye just leaves everyone blind."

I got up and ran into the ocean to rinse off the sand, jumping and down in the waist-high waves. The water was clear enough that I could see my feet hopping off the bottom and curious fish circling nearby.

"Jack, come in!" I called to him. No one else was on the beach. I wanted to make love in the water, reclaim the space from my bad thoughts. Afterward, we could sit under a thatched umbrella in one of the many outdoor restaurants on the shore and drink the day away. Drink Jane away. Drink Korea away. Drink all of it, and all of me, out to sea.

THE PERSIAN GULF

March 28, 2015

I sit down in the hospital pharmacy's waiting area with a copy of the *National* newspaper someone else has left behind. I want to get my pills and get out of here, but the pharmacist needs time to process my somewhat-contentious prescription. Four pharmacists are behind the counter, but mine is the one who spoke at length with my doctor on the phone. He pauses to confer with them every few minutes.

I'm supposed to be at a meeting with the chair from Chemical Engineering at my university. He wants to improve his department's web page. He's a grumpy, red-faced Englishman who'll bark orders at me. I heard one of my Muslim colleagues refer to him as a "problem drinker." I wonder if they ever say that about me? I take great pains to hide any sign of my drinking from them. I act chipper when I feel like shit. I smile when I feel like crying.

The Emiratis on campus are vastly more temperate, perhaps a byproduct of being teetotalers, than the Europeans and Americans. We're a mixed-gender campus, as well as being ethnically diverse. Unlike most other colleges in the region, men and women share the same classrooms too. This university defies every expectation and shatters every stereotype I had of the Middle East. In fact, this campus is almost a world of its own.

The president of the university is an American man who has an American female chief of staff. The vice president is an Emirati man, as is the head of procurement. An Emirati woman runs human relations. A Frenchman is in charge of campus facilities and construction. Our security guards are African men. The food retailers are Filipinas. Rocky, the young man who delivers my coffee to my desk twice a day, is from Sri Lanka.

Rocky is probably worried by my absence at the moment, just as my male supervisor from Palestine may be.

I text my boss, Ali, that I'm running late and should arrive on campus by eleven a.m.

No probs, he texts back. Tks.

I didn't tell a soul, not even my husband, where I was headed this morning. I hoped to get in, get my meds, and get out before I needed to say anything. But my plans are in danger of being thwarted by a lollygagging pharmacist.

I lift the newspaper up to cover my face, even though only a few other people are in the pharmacy waiting room. The front page features a story about the murder of an American teacher that took place in Abu Dhabi three months ago. I've been following the news closely because the crime hit so close to home in so many ways.

The murder happened on the ground floor of Sun and Sky Towers, across the street from our apartment in Mangrove Place. The circumstances were similar to Carolyn's death twenty-seven years earlier in Seoul—the victim having been stabbed to death by another female.

There was one striking difference, however. The culprit, a veiled and gloved Muslim woman, was in police custody forty-eight hours later. The residents and government of Abu Dhabi were outraged. The killer turned out to be a lone wolf, not part of a terrorist cell. Her trial was swift and she was sentenced to execution. No issues of jurisdiction stood in the way. The family of the victim would see justice soon and could even attend the execution if they so desired.

I lower the paper to see if any progress is being made on my medication. The pharmacist is typing information into his computer. I lean back in the chair and continue reading about the dead teacher. I can't help but wonder how Carolyn's family has managed in the decades since her death.

How have I managed, for that matter? Not particularly well, until meeting Allan. By then, eleven years after Carolyn's death, alcohol was an integral part of my identity as a party girl with a dark past.

THE ATLANTIC OCEAN

August 2, 1997

Allan and I married on the southern coast of Maine exactly one year after meeting at a bar in Burlington, Vermont. His sons, John and Andrew, ages fourteen and twelve, were our witnesses. After the ceremony, which took roughly twenty-three seconds, Allan and I sipped martinis on the front porch of the Cape Arundel Inn.

I'd moved to Vermont after spending five years in Phoenix, Arizona, with Jack, who turned out to be even more remote in the United States than he ever was in South Korea. And I had grown even more restless than I'd ever been. Jack and I were our own toxic cocktail.

"Do you want to get married?" I asked him at a bar near the border with Nevada. We'd been together for two years at that point. "We could drive to Las Vegas and do it tonight!"

"If you're looking to get married, then you've got the wrong guy," he said, as if we were on our first date and not a couple who'd lived through hell in Seoul.

I never looked at Jack the same again after that. I felt betrayed, enraged. Yet I stayed with him, punishing myself for his rejection and clinging to our past. Who else would know what it was like to have a friend murdered and to discover that an even better friend maybe killed her?

For the next two years, I went to happy hour almost every weeknight with my colleagues from the publishing company where I worked as an editor. Jack was in graduate school at Arizona State, getting a PhD in English literature. He spent his evenings writing papers on Edward Said and Michel Foucault in the library. On winter weekends he skied alone in the northern mountains while I danced at local nightclubs.

I drank beyond my standard capacity on those nights, doing shots of Sex on the Beach on top of beer and wine. Inebriated, I brought nameless men home while Jack was away. I lost count of how many drinks I had over the years and how many other men I slept with. But there was a final straw, and it broke me more than Jack.

I'd gone to Washington, DC, for a long weekend to visit a group of friends from Kenya who had jobs with international development agencies. I arrived on a day when the entire city—indeed, the entire country—was on pins and needles waiting to see if President Bill Clinton's first budget would pass Congress. The deciding vote lay in the hands of Bob Kerrey, a US senator from Nebraska and decorated veteran from the Vietnam War.

My friends took me for drinks at an Italian restaurant known as the hangout for political operatives, to watch televised coverage of the vote on the Senate floor.

The crowd went silent as Kerrey cast his vote. Was it yes or no?

Everyone erupted in cheers when we heard it was yes. The bartender opened a bottle of champagne and poured a glass for those of us sticking around to celebrate.

Just as I clinked glasses with my friends, I noticed a handsome older man in a suit and tie walk in the door. We locked eyes.

"That's Bob Kerrey," one of my friends said, noticing my stare. "The man who just voted to pass the president's budget."

In all the fuss about the vote, no one had mentioned how handsome the former governor of Nebraska was, with a lean runner's body and big blue eyes. Kerrey's charisma was as intoxicating as Cemal's when I'd first spied him in Dar es Salaam.

The senator walked to a small table on the other side of the room. I noticed he wasn't wearing a wedding band. He sat by himself, ordering from the menu. He was a bachelor, alone after an important night. The waiter delivered him a bottle of red wine and one glass.

I dared one of my friends to ask, on my behalf, for a taste of his wine. She approached Kerrey's table, and they spoke briefly, but she returned empty-handed.

A few minutes later, Kerrey stood up from the table, picked up the wine bottle, and walked toward me.

"Here you go," he said, putting it down on the table.

"What made you say yes?" I asked.

"To bringing the wine?"

"To the vote."

"Love."

"Of what?"

"My country."

I was pretty sure I was in love him with already. Six weeks later, we were in bed together in a hotel room in Minneapolis, after rendezvousing in the city for a picnic date on a hill overlooking the Mississippi River. I'd invited him, choosing Minnesota because it was midway between my residence in Arizona and his in Washington, DC.

I returned to Phoenix afterward and broke up with Jack, who was shocked that I wanted out of our relationship. I told him that I'd met someone else.

"He'll never love you like I do," he said as venomously as a cobra spits. Jack was half-right.

On my second date with Bob, in a hotel room in Chicago, he said the people of Nebraska would never understand our twenty-three-year age difference. I was devastated and drank all five of the tiny vodka bottles from the minibar after Bob fell asleep. The vodka diluted the feeling that

I wasn't good enough for a senator to love. But it also emboldened me to the idea that I didn't have to settle for the kind of love Jack was offering.

My best Peace Corps friend from Kenya, who was living in Burlington, Vermont, recommended small-city life as a cure for my doubly broken heart. Within weeks, I quit my job and moved across the country. I found an apartment with a view of Lake Champlain and proceeded to host a month-long pity party for myself. Invited guests were cheap wine, American Spirit cigarettes, and flannel pajamas. I spent two separate evenings in the local emergency room suffering from migraine headaches so severe I needed intravenous medicine to manage the crushing pain.

"You probably shouldn't drink alcohol or smoke," the doctors said, smelling both on me. "They're migraine triggers."

When I finally felt ready to interact with the world again, I accepted a date with a young man to whom I'd been introduced. We met for drinks at a local bar, where I ended up in conversation with an older man with wild gray hair, sitting next to me. His name was Allan Nicholls, and he made films with Robert Altman. The more Allan spoke, the more interested I was in his life, which had also included playing the lead in the Broadway musical *Hair* in 1969, back when I was five years old.

"How come you live in Vermont?" I asked.

"My boys are here. I'm divorced. I leave when there's work to do in New York or LA, but I come back to relax and spend time with my sons."

"Seems like you should be on a date with Raquel Welch in Malibu or something, not in this dive bar."

"I went on a blind date with Raquel Welch once in Malibu," he said, smiling and giggling. "I like this better. I'm looking for someone more like you."

A year later, facing the Atlantic Ocean, Allan and I vowed to love each other in sickness and health until death did us part.

THE PERSIAN GULF

March 28, 2015

I know I'm slowly killing myself. Drinking so much for so long is making me sick—not overtly, but I see the evidence mounting. I'm tired all the time, deep in my bones, enlivened only by the promise of the Holy Grail at day's end—a big goblet of booze in my hands at five p.m. on the dot.

My face is puffy, with cheeks like a chipmunk. The capillaries around my nose are broken and red. Whenever I get a manicure, the technician says my nails are soft and brittle. I'm so used to having a headache that I can't remember what it's like not to have one.

I overcompensate with tons of coffee, tons of makeup, and tons of Advil, and by buying increasingly larger-sized clothing. Gone is the dazzling girl who was lithe and full of life. All that's left in her swimmer's wake is a big dark shadow.

I've quit drinking for weeks and months at a time. But inevitably spent the whole period in self-imposed exile, counting down the days until I could resume. The longest I ever went was the nine months I was pregnant with David, when I was the head coach of women's swimming at James Madison University in Virginia.

Allan and I had moved to Harrisonburg from Burlington so I could take a shot at the new career path. One year into the gig, I still couldn't get my mind around the fact that I was the coach and not the swimmer. As soon as late-afternoon practices ended, I rushed home for my liquid reward.

My first two months of being pregnant and sober were tough. I conveniently blamed all my withdrawal symptoms—sleeplessness, thirst, nausea, hot flashes, and irritability—on being knocked up.

The worst side effect by far, however, was the amount of fear that surfaced when I couldn't rely on alcohol to keep it down. Very early on in the pregnancy, I experienced a panic attack in the middle of the night.

"I can't breathe! I can't breathe!" I shouted at Allan, who rushed me to the hospital, where the doctors decided to prescribe antidepressants for the remainder of my pregnancy.

I was afraid to sleep after the experience, afraid that I'd wake up in a panic all over again. When it was time to go to bed, Allan played his guitar and sang lullabies for me. Within a few weeks, the medicine picked up where Allan left off. I maintained a mostly even keel for the remaining seven months.

Still waiting for the pharmacist at Burjeel to give me the medicine that I've continued taking, I wonder what effect quitting alcohol permanently would have on me. Would I be happier? Would I be confused? Would I want to stay married?

I've lost touch with how I really feel about everything, including Allan. I love him and appreciate him. And there is no question that I love David with all of my heart and soul. But who am I, exactly? I feel like a robot programmed to travel and drink without thought or emotion. *Cheers to this place! Cheers to that one! Cheers to finding our way here! Cheers to going home! Cheers to saying "cheers"!*

What if nothing, including me, is ever cheerful again? What if staying alive isn't worth the effort?

BOULDER CREEK

October 15, 2008

David and I watched the 2008 Beijing Olympics swimming events in the comfort of our living room in Burlington, Vermont. I couldn't believe twenty years had passed since the Seoul Games and Carolyn's murder.

"That's my old race!" I yelled to David when the women swam the 50-meter freestyle.

"Mommy was in the Olympics!" David screamed, dancing around in his pajamas. Our house was lined with large glass windows from which to see Lake Champlain, reminiscent of my childhood fishbowl house in Florida.

"I only qualified for the Trials. But this is the race I liked to swim. I watched the Olympics in person when I lived in Korea. Not too far from Beijing."

I stopped short of saying that I once thought Korea looked like Siberia's penis. And I certainly didn't mention how the friend with whom I'd had the conversation was murdered three days later. Nor did

I tell my four-year-old how her divisive case came to resemble the split Korean landscape.

Justice for Carolyn was stuck in no-man's-land, much like the uninhabitable space known as the DMZ between North and South Korea. Carolyn's case was part of an unoccupied territory—stuck in a ceasefire instead of coming to a conclusion. No one could solve it, change it, or end it.

Watching the Beijing Games with David, I wondered if I could bring Carolyn's story out of limbo by writing about her. But doing so might put me in Jane's path. She was out there, somewhere in the United States, living her life.

"Liquid courage," I called the cocktails I sipped while trying to write about my experiences in Seoul and Carolyn's death after the 1988 Summer Olympic Games. Allan delivered more every hour or so, when I called out for more. He seemed glad that I was facing the horror of those days, and also seemed to recognize that I needed some fluid to get the gears going again.

I grappled at length with the central problem of telling the story: Jane had never been charged with the crime of killing Carolyn, even though her coconspirator, Marissa, had confessed their alleged actions in a Korean court of law. As far as American law was concerned, Jane was untouchable. She couldn't be accused, charged, or convicted in a US court. Maybe Marissa had been more involved than she'd let on; maybe Jane wasn't even involved. Maybe Jane was a model citizen. Maybe she had a daughter now. Maybe nothing was what it seemed, or what Marissa said it was.

I decided to track down Marissa. I wanted to hear her confession with my own ears. I found her quickly—she was teaching at a special high school near Denver. I sent her a short email about wanting to get together at some point to talk about Seoul and life ever since. She wrote back immediately, as if no time, or crime, had passed. She said she was eager to catch up and see me again. Her email was riddled with exclamation marks.

I was surprised by Marissa's exuberance. Did she think we'd gab about the good old days? Walk hand in hand down the boulevard? Why didn't she offer an apology in advance of a potential reunion? Or, at the very least, mention that she was looking forward to explaining everything in person? Her email made me wonder if Carolyn was actually alive and I'd drunkenly dreamt her murder. Oh, how I wished that had been the case.

Two weeks later, I flew to Denver to see Marissa in person. I'd told her in subsequent emails that I was coming through town on my way to Steamboat Springs, where my father and stepmother were vacationing. When she offered to make the three-hour drive with me so I'd have company in case the car broke down on the high mountain pass, I briefly wondered if Marissa was hoping for an opportunity to kill me. Maybe she'd been more involved in Carolyn's death than any of us knew. I'd read, on the Internet, all the news articles in Marissa's hometown paper about her incarceration in Seoul and her release. In each one, she told the same story about covering up the crime but couldn't explain why she'd done so. I'd also read everything I could find about Carolyn's case in international papers, including the English-language Korean ones. Same story everywhere I looked.

I arranged to meet Marissa in a public place and warned her that I could only stay for an hour or two before hitting the road *alone*. The truth was that I'd head back to the airport, and away from her, as soon as possible after I heard what she had to say. I didn't want to make the drive to see my father, who really was in Steamboat. The mission was to see Marissa and get home.

I showed up in the same condition I often showed up in at ELI in Seoul—red eyed and groggy from drinking the night before—although I looked far better than Marissa, whose front teeth were brown and rotted. Her once-bouncy strawberry-blonde hair had turned stringy and gray. Her clothes were old, hanging awkwardly on her hunched body. She seemed like a homeless woman acting as if things hadn't caved in on her.

We exchanged pleasantries for a minute or two. I told her I was married with a son. She said she was married with stepchildren. I asked after her mother, who I'd spoken with on the phone from Marissa's apartment in Seoul a few days after Carolyn's death. She'd called every day in the aftermath of the murder to see how Marissa was doing. I wondered what her reaction had been when Marissa confessed to being a part of the deception.

Using her mother as an entry point, I asked Marissa what it was like coming back to the States after spending a number of months in a Korean prison.

"I gave myself five years to recover," Marissa began hesitantly. "I saw a lot of therapists and finally found one that worked. An abuse expert. She helped me understand what happened to me."

What happened to her? She was acting like she'd been the victim. *Five years to recover?* She looked horrible. Marissa showed no discernable signs of recovery twenty years after the fact.

"What exactly *did* happen, Marissa?" I said softly.

"I wonder what version of the story you've heard."

I paraphrased what Kimberly had written to me about the crime, and what I'd read in newspapers.

"I'm glad that's what you heard," Marissa said, "because that's the truth."

"What do you remember about that night?"

"The last thing I remember is cleaning the knife. In the kitchen sink. I washed the blood off it."

"Whose sink?" I asked. "Yours or Carolyn's?"

She didn't remember. And she never saw the shirt and skirt again that she'd been wearing that night. She assumed that Jane had gotten rid of them.

"What happened to the knife?" I asked.

"I don't know. But the police ended up coming to take our knives from the apartment, which was a shame since I really liked some of them."

I'd seen her knives on top of her cupboard on Christmas Day. Had Jane put them there and told Marissa that the police had taken them? Or did the police take them later? Was the knife that killed Carolyn among the ones I saw? I didn't want to press Marissa for details, fearful that she might suffer some kind of psychic break right in front of me. I wanted to get as many facts as I could and then get to the airport. I'd drink all night on the red-eye flight back to the East Coast.

"What else do you remember?" I asked.

"Not much. I blocked so much," she said. "Then it got all mixed up in my mind. The police planted memories."

I briefly looked into my beer before drinking it all down in one long gulp.

"Still drinking like a fish!" Marissa laughed. "You always did. When I didn't hear from you after Seoul, I wondered if something bad happened to you. You were so wild."

I was not amused by her comment. I partially blamed my continued drinking on the horrible crime in which she'd ostensibly participated.

"Marissa," I said, lifting my head to look directly at her. "What I need to know is why you did such a thing. Why would you go back to Carolyn's apartment that night and why would you help cover up the crime? It doesn't make any sense."

"Because I'm too nice," she said quickly, angrily.

I felt sick to my stomach. I wanted to get up and run as fast as I could. Yet I stayed—trying to play nice too, until I couldn't stand Marissa's grotesque presence one second longer.

"We were in a foreign country," she continued. "I wasn't sure what was going to happen. Jane needed my help. I couldn't just abandon her."

"So you helped Jane that night for whatever reason. Maybe you were scared. But why didn't you run to the police the next day, or come to me, or anyone?"

"Nancy, you know me, I don't run from things," she responded without a trace of irony. "I wasn't scared."

I wanted to tell her that, in fact, I didn't know her. And that there were times when it's more appropriate to run, like if your roommate comes home with blood on her hands after killing a mutual friend.

"Besides, once I was involved, it was too late. I was part of it then," she added, softly hitting her forehead with her fist. "I was so stupid. So stupid. So stupid."

I asked Marissa what had happened after the truth came out, after she'd confessed. She said that everyone avoided her, and she was living alone in a *yogwan* hotel downtown awaiting trial. Her prison sentence came almost as a relief, she said. She had company at last.

"Everyone fixates on how awful it must have been," she explained, "but I try to take away the positives. I met some wonderful Korean people."

I realized that Marissa hadn't mentioned anyone else's difficult experience, most notably Carolyn's family. What about how awful it was for them? And no doubt still was, considering the lack of justice—a situation for which Marissa might be partially to blame.

"What were you charged with?" I asked.

"Concealing evidence and harboring a criminal."

"Even though a criminal hadn't actually been charged?"

"Yes, that's what my family and lawyer argued in my defense."

"When did you get out of prison?"

"I got out early. After five months instead of six years."

"It must have been nice to get home and be with your family again."

"Yeah, and, hey, I wrote to you. The letter got sent back."

"I kind of remember that. I got a postcard, but I recall returning a letter to you. I couldn't deal with it then. I'm sorry."

Why was I apologizing? Marissa didn't seem to regret—or even acknowledge—why I might not have wanted to hear from her. She treated the whole matter as if she'd done the right thing and everybody else misunderstood her intentions.

"Did you ever speak to Jane again?" I asked, trying to redirect the conversation.

"When I got back, the US Attorney asked me to wear a wire and see if I could get her to confess."

"Oh my God," I said. "How did it go?"

"She just kept saying, 'I don't know what you're talking about.'"

"Were you scared?"

"Not really."

"Did you ever speak to her again?"

"No."

I asked our server for the bill and paid it. I stood up to indicate that our time together was over. We hugged and walked in separate directions. I never contacted or spoke with Marissa again. But I continued to wonder if Marissa might be fabricating details about what happened that night. She certainly seemed unhinged by the events surrounding Carolyn's death, but I was uncertain about her ability to distinguish reality from fantasy.

When I returned home, the FBI files I'd requested through the Freedom of Information Act were waiting for me. I opened them quickly, horrified to see that each page was stamped with the phrase "armed and dangerous" in reference to Jane. There was no way in hell I was going to track her down for a conversation.

But I did reach out to one of the US Attorneys who'd sought possible ways to prosecute Jane. He and I spoke at length on the phone.

"I still don't understand why she can't at least be tried," I said.

"The crime happened on Korean soil, not American land. The Koreans are the only ones who can accuse, try, and prosecute her," he explained, clearly still troubled by the details of the case.

"Even though neither the victim nor the alleged perpetrator was Korean?" I asked.

"The location of the crime determines jurisdiction, not the nationalities of those involved," he answered. "I'm sorry, Nancy. I know it's not what you want to hear, but that's how the law works. The alleged murderer in this can't even be charged, let alone brought to trial."

"I was thinking of contacting Jane, to ask her what happened myself."

"Nancy, I encourage you to proceed with extreme caution. You've read the files. There's nothing to be accomplished by confronting her. You won't win."

He'd used the magic words. Pursuing Jane was an unwinnable race, and there most certainly was the possibility that she wasn't Carolyn's killer. I had to let her go, just like my Olympic dreams.

THE PERSIAN GULF

March 28, 2015

I place the newspaper on the chair next to me and try to see if the pharmacist is any closer to having my medication ready. There are no signs of life behind the counter. He must have gone in a back room to get the goods, which could mean that I'm closer to the end of this race.

I wonder how many people have died in this hospital. Muslims, Jews, Hindus, Buddhists, Christians from all over the world. No doubt some of them had been victims of crime, Alzheimer's disease, or substance abuse. Regardless of nationality or cause of death, we all go back to the Earth one day. Ashes to ashes. Dust to dust.

My father died three years ago in a hospital in Naples, Florida. He'd tanked rapidly in memory care, losing his ability to walk and talk. The day he no longer recognized me—his gal—was devastating. Very soon thereafter, he contracted a penicillin-resistant infection and our family agreed it was time to let him go.

My stepmother, Nora, who'd been happily married to my dad for thirty years, had watched him disintegrate before her eyes. She was as crushed by the disease as he'd been—bearing the enormous weight of seeing the man she loved disappear into thin air.

My brother, Lee, a lieutenant with the Tampa Police Department, managed the duration of our father's illness with the same kind of resiliency and forbearance he used in his detective work, and had used in his youth. Even as a kid, Lee managed difficult situations by staying distant. While I complained about my parents, my brother played with Hot Wheels. Distraction was his best defense.

He visited our father as often as possible, asking all the right questions of the doctors and helping Nora with logistics. I was proud of the man my brother had become—temperate in all things, even alcohol consumption.

My stepsister Kathy, a nurse in North Carolina, helped her mom with medical advice over the phone. She visited Beau and Nora as often as she could. Kathy supported me too, whenever I felt badly about being in Vermont while so much was happening in Florida with my father's health. I wished for more chances to see him, but at the same time I was afraid I'd have to make good on an oath he'd forced me to take ten years earlier.

"Promise me something, gal," he'd said from his recliner. There was a baseball game on television, but he'd been reading an article in the *New England Journal of Medicine*.

"Anything," I answered.

"Swear on your grandmother's Bible that you will put a gun to my head if I wind up like my father."

He was dead serious.

I didn't want to say yes, but his intensity was intimidating and his fear palpable. He'd spent his entire career as a neurologist taking care of patients with Alzheimer's, and he loathed the illness's progression. My dad could hear the disease coming for him, like a Doppler effect, and wanted to be able to stop it—with my help.

"Swear to me," he repeated, seeing my hesitation.

He collected guns and kept them under lock and key. He knew I could shoot them, because he'd taught me how.

I put my hand on the leather-bound King James Bible that had belonged to my great-grandmother Nannie Dunlap and my grandmother Nancy Scott, and swore to kill my own father if Alzheimer's came to call.

I didn't kill him in the end, but I did let him die. My family put him in hospice and let the infection run its course. Within five days, his body caught up with his brain and he was completely gone.

That night, I lay in a hotel bed and drank two bottles of cheap wine from the nearby gas station. The Sea of Lonely in me raged like a hurricane. I held on to the mattress as if it were a dinghy and to the wine as if it were a buoy. Great waves of sadness washed over me—despair over what had been, and fear for what was yet to come. My dad had started showing signs of his father's disease at age sixty. Both men died at the age of seventy-three. Did my brain have only about two decades left?

Sitting in Abu Dhabi's Burjeel Hospital now, four years later, I'm down to about fifteen years of actually being able to hold on to my memories if Alzheimer's is headed my way. But I probably won't last that long if I keep destroying my own brain cells with alcohol. Which is a better way to go? Either way, I won't have to remember the trauma of this day and so many others.

THE SOUTH CHINA SEA

January 15, 2010

Becoming a mother turned my wanderlust to dust. I could barely overcome my fears for David's safety in order to get to the grocery store for wine—the magic potion that quelled my anxiety—let alone an airport or another country. I left my coaching job at James Madison a few months after David was born so we could move back to Vermont. Still, a part of me longed for the day when I'd feel safe enough to show my son the wonders of the world. I doubted that that time would ever come.

Just before David turned six, in 2010, Allan was offered a position teaching film at an American graduate school in Singapore.

"What do you think?" he asked.

"Singapore is the safest place in the world. Let's go."

And so we did. But Singapore had a surprise for me: alcohol was cost prohibitive. A Singapore Sling at the famed Raffles Hotel was almost $30.

The government puts an exorbitant tax on alcohol to discourage its use. Singapore wants citizens to be productive members of society, not addicts. Tourists and expats pay a high price for their vices. Allan earned a sizeable salary, but it barely covered the cost of living in one of the most expensive cities in the world. We had to watch every penny.

We limited ourselves to having drinks on the weekend. But I spent weeknights obsessing about Friday. Every Sunday, I faced the grim reality of being dry and antsy for the subsequent five days. I convinced myself that having none was better than having just one, because I'd never been able to drink a single glass without wanting more. I didn't feel any withdrawal symptoms during the week, only the need to make time pass more quickly. The reward for doing so was a martini and bottle of wine in our living room on Friday evening and again on Saturday. Allan's colleagues would come over too, and bring their booze with them. I never had to worry about running out on those nights. Still, I felt compelled to drink as much as I could to compensate for the dry days to come, like a camel.

Being frugal helped us save up enough money to take a cheap ferry ride to the nearby island of Bintan, Indonesia, to celebrate Chinese New Year. Only an hour by boat, Bintan felt worlds away from Singapore in terms of strict culture and high prices. A two-night stay at the "Cheery Family Resort" was cheaper than one drink at Raffles. And the local Bintang Beer was less than a dollar per bottle. I was free to go overboard.

On the first day of our mini vacation, Allan and I sat by the enormous hotel pool enjoying cold beverages while David was entertained in the Kids' Club nearby. We enjoyed dinner that night in one of the hotel restaurants with a view of the shimmering South China Sea and two bottles of remarkably affordable wine.

"David, I was born somewhere out there." I pointed toward the horizon, where the sea met the sky.

"In the water?"

Allan and I giggled. "On another chain of islands," I answered. "The Philippines."

The next morning, I took David down to the pool for a swim while Allan checked his email in the business center. David was already a good swimmer, having had lessons at the YMCA since he was two, but I liked to work on his strokes with him.

We arrived poolside in the midst of a crisis. A boy about David's age was sprawled out on the deck. His mother was pleading for him to "stay strong" while pool attendants performed CPR. Within a minute or two, the child was whisked away on a gurney with his mother running behind him. We never knew whether he lived or died. The whole thing happened so fast I couldn't even process it. I spent the entire afternoon in tears, ordering beer after beer from the pool bar. I couldn't consume enough to wash away what I'd seen.

Arriving back in Singapore on Sunday afternoon, I bought a bottle of vodka at the small duty-free shop in the port.

"Less expensive here," I told Allan, who wasn't happy that I had done so.

"I thought we weren't drinking during the week," he said.

"You didn't see that boy," I snapped. "I'm drinking."

For the first time, Allan looked frustrated with me, disappointed, even.

"You don't get to decide how we spend our money," I raged.

"It's not the money, Nancy," he responded.

"I've hardly drunk at all since being here, if that's what you're implying," I said with the same stone-cold stare I'd perfected behind the blocks before a big race.

"I'm not implying anything, Nancy. I just think it's good to take breaks. Good for our finances and our health."

In defiance, I drank my vodka throughout the following week. I also stocked up on a relatively cheap brand of Australian wine at a grocery store near David's kindergarten and drank that too. Alcohol had a new job: keeping thoughts of the dead boy at bay.

I also amped up my mission to make sure David was an excellent swimmer. In the big pool at our condo, I showed him how to float on his back by filling his belly up with air.

"You're your own flotation device," I said. "You have to save yourself in this world."

THE PERSIAN GULF

March 28, 2015

I can't stand one more minute of waiting at Burjeel, but the pharmacist never seems to tire of moving at a snail's pace from his computer to the pill shelf and back again. I want to tell him that he's reached the acceptable limit of dawdling. Yet I can't risk the last few seconds of this tenuous transaction. I have to hold out until those pills are in my hand.

The clock hanging over the shelves of skin-whitening makeup and Moroccan hair oils indicates that I've only been waiting for fifteen minutes. I was certain that at least an hour had passed. I'm not as tuned in to time as I once was.

I get up from my chair to examine the selections of creams and lotions. There's a special SPF 50 sunscreen for sensitive skin. Since coming to Abu Dhabi, I've been using sunblock by the gallon, trying, in vain, to stop myself from turning into a raisin. Reaching out for the fancy bottle, I notice dark spots covering my hands. Not once has it occurred to me to apply sunscreen there. My hands look as if they belong to an old lady, not someone on the brink of fifty.

I managed to make a home for my family in this foreign uterus-shaped town. I found the resolve to keep putting David on an unnamed bus for the American school. I made a good living at an Arab university. But I completely neglected to protect my hands from the sun.

Who forgets their hands, especially someone who uses them to pour booze every night? What's more, they're swollen. I yank off my wedding band with the help of some lotion from a tester bottle. There are deep indentations in my ring finger. What could I blame it on other than alcohol?

Heat-related dehydration? Maybe. I could drink more water.

Menopausal bloating? Possibly. I could increase my fiber intake.

Weight gain? Yes, as the scales corroborated. I should start dieting immediately.

Excess salt? Perhaps I need a diuretic.

I put the sunscreen back on the shelf and get a cup of coffee from the complimentary kiosk. I come back to the real question at hand: How long have I been drinking heavily? When and where was the turning point? Since arriving in Abu Dhabi? Since David was born? Since Korea? Since Kenya? Since college?

I realize that *Since high school* is the answer. Thirty-three years ago, minus the nine months I was pregnant with David. The first time I got drunk was at a friend's house, in ninth grade, with two other girls. We opened her parents' liquor cabinet and played strip poker. When the four of us were completely drunk and naked, we streaked through the neighborhood. We spent the rest of the night wrapped in bath towels and throwing up. The experience was enough to turn my pals off alcohol altogether.

But I knew immediately that I liked the liberating effects of booze, even if I had to pay for it later. The trick, as I came to learn, was finding the sweet spot between intoxication and inebriation. Balancing on that fine line minimized the unpleasant side effects, whether that evening or the next morning. Since then, my drinking has spanned neighborhoods and oceans, nakedness, and sicknesses.

Self-loathing begins to rise in me, like bile. I try to push it into the deep abyss that lurks far under my surface. But my emotions are a seesaw: I push one down and another pops up. I feel enraged by my situation this morning, but am calmed by thoughts of the solution that arrives every day at five p.m.

THE DEAD SEA

February 12, 2015

I considered foregoing our trip to the ancient city of Petra after a Jordanian fighter pilot was killed—burned alive in a cage—by ISIS militants in Syria. But when the Jordanian government launched a decisive counterattack, I figured it was as good a time as any to travel to the country.

David and I were the only Westerners on the Royal Jordanian flight from Abu Dhabi to Amman. Not a word was spoken in English, nor written in the newspapers that were handed out. In fact, very few words were spoken in any language. The plane was eerily silent. Not one comment came out of the cockpit during the three-hour flight. I tried to order a glass of wine, but the flight attendant shook her head. There was no booze on board. I had Ativan for situations like this. I took one.

Hunkered down in our seats, David and I sporadically whispered about his "relationship" with a classmate named Natasha, a Russian Orthodox expat from Kazakhstan. Even at the tender age of ten, they were considering elevating their status to "dating." But when David hedged on the idea, Natasha freaked out. So instead of becoming a pair, they had a falling-out. David couldn't understand how everything had gotten so mixed up. He'd been tearful for days and seemed especially so on the silent flight.

I hoped a new place would give him greater perspective on the universal problem of love and loss, although I've never understood the human tendency to compare hardships. How could anyone be made happier by hearing news of someone in a far worse situation? Maybe the simple act of being with others would help my son feel better. We could be anywhere in the world, but it would be Jordan for Valentine's Day weekend.

Upon landing in Amman, David and I both took notice of an extremely elderly Jordanian woman trying to navigate the plane's aisle with a huge box of Legos. Concerned about how she'd get down the stairs to the tarmac, I put my arm out for her to take. We walked down the treacherous steps through wind and sleet. David followed behind with her small carry-on bag and our backpacks, the other passengers treading slowly behind him. I felt like we were leading a parade, or perhaps a funeral procession—the box of Legos serving as flag, cross, and casket.

Safe from the elements in a bus bound for the main terminal, the old lady nodded at me with a playful smile. I suspected that those Legos might be for her own amusement, not a grandchild's. I smiled back.

After clearing immigration, David and I easily located our representative from the tour company. My first email exchange with the office manager, a few weeks earlier, had been reassuring.

"Jordan is safe, and we will take care of you," a woman named Amira wrote to me.

She said her best guide would be waiting for us with a sign at baggage claim. And we found him instantly. Neatly dressed and smiling, with big brown eyes and a crisp, clear command of English, he introduced himself as "Allah."

"Allah" handed me a mobile phone. He said we could use it at any time for anything and that his cell and home numbers were on speed dial.

"Press 1 for Allah. Press 2 for Allah."

"But there is only one Allah," I said, regretting it immediately. I hadn't meant to joke about a central tenet of the Quran.

Fortunately, our "Allah" laughed mightily. "That's right, Nancy, but my name is Ala'a," he said, spelling it out.

On the forty-five-minute drive from the airport to our hotel, Ala'a quizzed us on Jordanian history. He had to answer his own questions, because David and I were clueless.

What was the name of Amman under the Roman Empire? *Philadelphia.*

What does Petra mean? *Rock.*

How many Syrian refugees are living here? *750,000.*

"Tell us about the Dead Sea, Ala'a," I said, unable to bear the thought of so many displaced families.

"I will show you the pillar of salt that is believed to be Lot's wife, who fled from Sodom when God sent fire and brimstone. She was told not to look back, but she did. Before its ruin, Sodom was like the Garden of Eden. Afterward, the valley filled with water and became the Dead Sea."

As our car descended below sea level into the Jordan Rift Valley, I felt pressure in my ears as if I were diving into the deep end of a pool.

"I'll pick you up at eight a.m.," Ala'a said, dropping us off at the hotel after his car was checked for explosives at the gate. "It's three hours to Petra from here. Sleep well. *Salaam.*"

David and I sat down on couches in the glass lobby that faced the body of water I'd come to see.

"How about a plate of spaghetti, David?" I asked. We needed a break from hummus. I needed a drink too, but it was still early, and I always waited till the appointed hour.

Sand and sleet took turns blocking the view of the Dead Sea, which I estimated to be about four football fields away from where we sat. The water appeared to be lashing the shores as if the city of Sodom were still being punished.

"Let's make some valentine cards," I suggested after lunch.

"Not one for Natasha," David responded.

"We'll make one for her, and then you can decide later if you want to give it to her."

The only supplies we could procure from the front desk were a pencil and a big piece of brown cardboard.

After settling into our hotel room, David began tearing the cardboard into two-inch-by-two-inch pieces. I stopped myself from turning on CNN. I didn't want to know about any more death and destruction caused by ISIS. David and I were only one hundred kilometers south of the Syrian border.

"Tell me more about your conversation with Natasha," I asked David. "What really happened?"

He got teary again. "She said she loved me and I didn't answer."

"How come?"

"I don't know. I don't know anything about love yet. I said something dumb instead."

"I say dumb stuff all the time. Maybe that doesn't help you right now, but it's good to know that you aren't the first or last one to feel confused by love. And by the way, I love you more than anyone or any place in the whole world."

"I know, Mommy."

The storm continued to rage over the Dead Sea as David wrote notes on each hand-torn valentine card—the pencil lead almost too light to show up on the dark cardboard.

I felt an old surge of deep loneliness while watching him and the weather outside. I'd named the feeling "Sea of Lonely" during my father's illness. The phrase applied to the faraway look in my dad's eyes as well as the isolation I felt from my own long-lost identity. Neither of us bore any resemblance to the people we'd been during the swim meets of my youth.

A psychiatrist had tried to help me navigate the sensation by offering a metaphorical alternative to being swept away.

"Come sit on the shore with me and we'll watch the water ebb and flow together," she said.

Therapy turned into my first-ever distance event. We let sadness run its slow course. But seeing the Dead Sea brought the Sea of Lonely back to life.

"David," I said. "I want to go down to the water's edge."

"Right now?" he asked.

"Yes, before the sky is totally dark. Put your jacket on, over two shirts."

The big blue eyes behind David's black glasses looked perplexed—which I found preferable to his sadness. I feared that his reaction to Natasha meant that he had the Sea of Lonely inside too.

"Afterward we can go to the gift shop and get a souvenir," I added.

I wrapped up as best I could too. Jordan was fifty degrees colder than Abu Dhabi. We weren't prepared for the weather, let alone the emotions, in which we'd found ourselves.

We left the hotel via the glass doors to the swimming pools. Signs pointed us in the direction of the beach. The wind was so loud that I had to yell for David to hear me.

"This way," I said, taking his right hand in my left. We leaned into the gale-force winds and made our way across the three pool decks and down five flights of stairs before arriving a few dozen steps from the water. The sand whipping around made it almost impossible to see or communicate with each other. The sun was low on the horizon, casting a supernatural glow on the violent waves. I'd expected the Dead Sea to be more, well, lifeless.

The terrifying image before us made me think that God was still angry with all of us. He'd never quite recovered from Sodom, but seeing the world in even greater shambles made him want to slap the water over and over again.

"Change the name," David shouted at the top of his lungs.

"What?" I shouted back, cupping my ear near his mouth.

"The Harsh Sea!"

"No swimming for us!" I answered.

"What?"

"No swimming in the Harsh Sea!" I repeated. "You have to stay up here with me. We're just watching it! We're safe on shore! We don't have to get swept away!"

David smiled wide enough to get some sand in his mouth. "I wasn't going to swim, Mom!"

"Me either!" I laughed. "I love you, David!"

Within minutes, we were soaked from the Dead Sea's salty spray and the pouring rain. Maybe we were being blessed with holy water, in buckets.

Drenched and chilled, David and I began the trek back to the hotel. The wind pushed hard against us, but we tucked our heads and pressed ahead. Part of me wanted to run, like Lot's wife, away from the watery destruction behind us. But running would be dangerous.

We walked slowly across the slippery pool deck, dodging airborne lounge chairs. I tightened my grip on David's hand, which I hadn't released since starting our pilgrimage ten minutes earlier.

Dripping wet, we stopped in the pitiful lobby gift shop. Postcards were covered in dust; faded T-shirts hung on rusty racks. The clerk stared at David and me as if we were sailors back from a watery grave.

David found a deck of cards and a pack of gum, both of which I charged to our room. We went upstairs to change and returned to the huge velvet couches in the lobby for a round of Go Fish. An older British couple sat on the other side of the expansive room, sipping their cocktails. I ordered one too, along with a bottle of wine to go.

Settling into our hotel room for the night, I locked the doors and drew the curtains. I opened the bottle of wine and put it on the bedside table along with a plastic cup from the bathroom. I called Allan.

"This hotel is forlorn, or forsaken, or something. I can't find the words for it." I said, without bothering to even say hello. "There's a terrible storm outside. Unearthly. Winds like I've never seen. It's making me sad, for some reason. David is sad too. Did you know this area was Sodom? Maybe that's why we're sad. I don't know."

"Nancy," Allan interrupted. "I Googled your hotel to see where it was and found out something bad happened there a few years back. They had to close down, made major upgrades, and reopened again under a new name. It's supposed to be fine now. I'm sure you're fine."

"Do you know what happened, exactly?"

"Yeah. I wasn't going to tell you until you got home."

"What?"

"A mother and a son died while staying there."

My stomach did a backflip.

"How?"

"A sickness. Unclear about what it was," Allan answered.

"I think I'll call Ala'a."

"God?"

I laughed, glad for the comic relief. "Our driver. Spelled A-L-A-A. He gave me a cell phone and said I could reach him on speed dial. Two speed dials, actually."

"Well, sounds like you're in good hands." Allan sounded relieved. "Turn on the news, if you can. Some Coptic Christians in Libya have been killed by ISIS."

"I've had enough bad news," I said, finally starting to feel the Sea of Lonely recede. "Besides, I have something good to report."

"And what is that?"

"The Dead Sea is alive and well."

THE PERSIAN GULF

March 28, 2015

"Nanshee Bershaw," the pharmacist says over the sound system. "Your prescription is ready."

I startle, even though I've been anticipating this moment for what feels like ages. I spill the last bit of my coffee on my skirt, and it runs down my calves into my right boot.

"Nanshee Bershaw, your prescription is ready."

"One moment!" I call out, annoyed that the pharmacist is now rushing me. I quickly pull my boot off and dab at my foot with my beverage napkin. I'm surprised to see the tattoo on my right calf. It's always covered unless I'm swimming. I also have a brightly colored mermaid on my forearm, which is hidden by my long-sleeved shirts. My Abu Dhabi university has a policy against body art being displayed in the workplace.

My ankle tattoo features two coordinates in black ink: the latitude and longitude of my birthplace in the Philippines; the latitude and longitude of the Military Demarcation Line between North and South Korea. The latter represented the split in my life after Carolyn's death.

The coordinates of my death would complete the story. If I keep drinking at my current rate, that location could very well be Abu Dhabi.

I put my boot back on and walk quickly toward the counter.

"Please have a seat," the pharmacist says. "Let's go over the instructions for taking this medicine properly."

"Okay, but I've been taking it for more than eleven years."

He proceeds nonetheless. "Take it at the same time every day. Take it with water. Don't drink alcohol."

"What happens if I drink alcohol?" I ask, although I've Googled that answer a dozen times.

"The medicine can increase the side effects of drinking, make you sleepy or dizzy."

I nod.

"More importantly," he continues, "alcohol decreases the effectiveness of this medication. They cancel each other out. One is a depressant, the other is an antidepressant."

I nod.

"This is a thirty-day supply. Do you have any questions?"

I don't.

"May I have your insurance card?"

I hand him proof of my coverage. I notice that his paperwork says I'm Samoan. I laugh. Surely I look more like a Viking.

I pick up the bottle of pills. The warning label on the side is written in English and in Arabic. There's a small martini icon crossed out by a single diagonal line, like a tiny DMZ between two opposing forces. People on antidepressants should not drink. People south of the thirty-eighth parallel shouldn't go north of it. End of story.

By continuing to blur the line between medicine and alcohol, I'm walking into a land mine of my own making. And sooner or later, I'm going to blow myself up.

I need an armistice agreement like the one between North and South Korea: *Nancy Bercaw the Drinker hereby promises to halt the attacks on Nancy Bercaw the Depressant in exchange for peace in the region.* The Korean War Armistice Agreement, signed July 27, 1953, uses the term *belligerents* to describe the warring factions. The word could easily apply to both sides of me as well.

But I'm reluctant to end my war. I like being in the numb comfort zone of antidepressants and alcohol. I like no-man's-land. I don't know how to operate with a clear head. In fact, I'm terrified of sobriety and reality.

After David was born, I was overwhelmed by the prospect of keeping him safe. A little wine in the evening after he fell asleep helped push back the fear. The older he got, the more wine I needed for the increasing threats against us both. But now, in the Middle East, I see that my need to drink is probably making my son less safe. Maybe Abu Dhabi is the right time and place to stop. Here, surrounded by peaceful nondrinking Bedouins.

I could use the very same focus that helped me qualify for the Olympic Trials to face off against my liquid foes. The race takes shape in my head.

Bercaw in Lane 4.

Wine in Lane 5.

Vodka in Lane 3.

But I'll have to go the distance for the rest of my life, not just 23.69 seconds. The starting block is right here and now. Will I step up?

THE RIVER NILE

March 12, 2015

The kings of ancient Egypt were triumphant during their time on Earth *and* in the afterlife, explained our guide Mikail.

"Warriors in both places," he said. "That's the story they tell us through art and architecture."

Far more fascinating, to me, was Mikail's history. Shortly after picking us up at Cairo's airport, he mentioned being a Coptic Christian. David raised his eyebrows, because we'd seen the news in Jordan about the twenty-one Coptic Christians in Libya who were beheaded by ISIS terrorists.

The Copts, as they are called, believe Christ was a real man *and* a divine incarnation—two distinct beings, neither split nor divided, in one body. They've remained steadfast in their beliefs despite nonstop attempts to convert and destroy them over the centuries.

After spending the morning at the Sphinx and Great Pyramids in Giza, Mikail and our driver headed south to Sakkara, home to the oldest pyramid still standing in Egypt. Our journey included three police checkpoints, complete with machine guns and barbed wire.

At each stop, I heard Mikail tell the police, in Arabic, that his passengers were Canadian. But most of the focus actually seemed to be on him. Mikail was repeatedly asked to show work papers proving his status as a tour guide. He frequently touched his beard, which led me to believe that it might be the actual source of our delay.

Mikail's beard and mustache were full but impeccably groomed—a style favored by members of the Muslim Brotherhood. In the Middle East and North Africa, a man's facial hair can be a marker of political and religious affiliations. For a while, all beards were banned in Egypt for reasons similar to gang colors being banned on clothes and hats in American public schools. The sight of either could be interpreted as aggressive.

"Why don't you shave it off?" I asked Mikail after the third round of interrogations. Perhaps he was relying on his beard to look more like an oppressor than one of the oppressed? But there was nothing ominous about him. I wanted to get inside Mikail's mind more than the dead heads of pharaohs.

"Because it's fashionable," he smiled, a mouthful of gleaming white teeth. I wondered if he'd had the same procedure I tried in Abu Dhabi, but managed to steer clear of coffee for the proper period of time.

Mikail was a young, modern, unmarried man who worked predominantly with European tourists. He wore skinny jeans, pointed shoes, and a leather jacket. His English was perfect. He held a bachelor's degree in tourism. He was quite striking, and his contradictions mimicked Egypt's landscape, where the Nile flowed north.

The traffic in Cairo was far more unsettling than its police checkpoints, even with Mikail's ominous beard. Not one of the city's seven million inhabitants, who all seemed to drive at once, used a turn signal. Instead, they honked nonstop, weaving in and out of unmarked lanes. The drive to Sakkara felt more dangerous than anything I'd experienced in the Middle East to date. The fact that I was feeling particularly rough from bottom-shelf vodka and cheap wine at our hotel the night before didn't help.

I'd gone to the lobby bar, after our harrowing ride in from the airport, with David, who was eager for a Shirley Temple and a snack. I hoped we could sit in the lounge and play cards, but a group of tipsy international businessmen and their local counterparts made me uncomfortable. They looked me up and down as if they hadn't seen a woman for months and certainly not a blonde one. David and I quickly retreated to our room, where I bolted the door and ordered room service. Drunk men and foreign countries were a dangerous mix. Even David sensed it.

"That was creepy, Mommy."

I'd visited Egypt briefly in 1989, on my way back to the United States from Kenya, and was the subject of much unwanted attention then. I wasn't able to walk by myself in broad daylight, let alone sit in a bar, without being touched inappropriately. Except for a quick day-time visit to the Great Pyramids, I'd spent most of my time at a youth hostel with other Western women traveling alone. We'd shared a bottle of whiskey and played cards in the reception area. There were wrought-iron bars on every window, which made us feel more like prisoners than protected guests.

I was glad David and I had Mikail and a driver to take care of us. For some reason, Mikail's beard made me feel safer. Nobody was gonna fuck with someone who looked like he was with the Muslim Brotherhood, even if he was a Coptic Christian. The traffic seemed far more likely to kill us.

Nearing Sakkara, our driver abruptly careened onto a dirt side road, where he deftly navigated between bikes and pedestrians, as well as other oncoming vehicles, in an effort to cut time off our journey. I gasped loudly and grabbed my stomach.

"Don't worry," Mikail said, numbed to his city's chaotic and reck-less streets. "This is Egypt!"

I told Mikail that I needed a restroom. He signaled the driver to pull over. We jumped out of the van and Mikail took my hand, a violation of Muslim decency laws. He led me through the darting traffic and into a restaurant hidden behind a row of trucks.

Mikail spoke to the owner in Arabic, and I was given access to a surprisingly nice toilet where I promptly deposited the contents of my bowels. Meanwhile, David sat in the van with the driver as cars hurtled at breakneck speed around them. The aftermath of my drinking had put David in harm's way.

Back in the van, Mikail distracted us with tales of Imhotep—the high priest of architecture, engineering, and medicine, who'd designed King Djoser's sarcophagus at Sakkara. Pulling into the empty parking lot, we had an unrestricted view of the impressive necropolis.

Mikail led us to a patch of pristine camel-colored sand, which he used as a drawing board. He made a small-scale map of Sakkara with his finger, pointing out the highlights contained therein. A beggar walked past us, putting out his hand and then withdrawing it. He was so used to getting nothing, because so few people came to Sakkara, that he thwarted his own efforts. Mikail said that the tourist trade had died down after the Arab Spring in 2010 and had yet to make a comeback.

We proceeded to Djoser's tomb, which looked like a defunct stairway to heaven, where Mikail explained the process of mummification and its implications in the afterlife.

"The organs are removed and put inside canopic jars."

I shivered, even though sweat was dripping into my eyes and down my lower back.

"Say that again," I asked.

"The organs went into canopic jars. The stomach, intestines, lungs, and liver," he continued. "The heart stayed inside the body. When the king gets to the afterlife, the gods weigh his heart against the feather of truth. If it is light, then he can enter heaven. If it is heavy, a monster eats it."

I hugged Mikail, much to his surprise. "Thank you! Thank you so much! For bringing us here! This is perfect. Just what I needed."

I proceeded to tell Mikail the story of my father, whose obsession with Alzheimer's had led him to become a neurologist. When his own father had succumbed to the disease, my dad had asked the coroner to remove my grandfather's brain and put it in a jar. The contents of his head sat, like a crystal ball, in the middle of my father's office desk.

"David!" I said, dancing a jig in the sand. "I think your grandpa was a modern-day ancient Egyptian!"

David giggled. Mikail smiled. We were an overly delighted triumvirate for such a grim discussion in the middle of a barren landscape.

I told Mikail that *Brain in a Jar* was the title of a book I'd written about my father and me. And I explained how travel was meant to provide David with something outside himself, beyond our family history, from which to build a worldview. I wanted my son to have a huge window into the lives of others instead of a glass jar through which to gaze upon his ancestors' organs.

But what was my world built on? The contents of another kind of glass container filled with a liquid that was slowly pickling my insides. Would my son write *Liver in a Jar* about me one day?

Back at the hotel, I called room service while David took a shower.

"Two plates of spaghetti and a bottle of water," I said.

"Anything else, madam?"

"No. I mean yes." I tried to stop myself from saying anything else.

"A sweet, perhaps?"

"No." I willed myself to hang up the phone, but I couldn't.

"A vodka martini," I said, rolling my eyes.

"Anything else?

"Yes, a bottle of chardonnay."

THE PERSIAN GULF

March 28, 2015

The pharmacist finally puts the medication in front of me. I want to grab his hand, not because I'm eager to rip the bottle out of it, but because I need a human connection. I want to change the course of my life, right here, right now, but I'm not sure how. Maybe if I sit with him for the rest of the day I'll be okay.

My mind is already racing to happy hour at five p.m., when I always sit down with a martini to watch Becky Anderson, Abu Dhabi–based host of CNN's *Connect the World*. She'll tell me how the situation in Syria and Yemen is far worse than what I endured during an hour at Burjeel Hospital this morning. At least, that's what I'll hear her say.

The issues in the Middle East will give me an excuse to pour a second martini. I'll order a pizza for my son when I switch to drinking wine. I'll drop any empty bottles down the trash chute at Mangrove Place so Allan can't see how much I've had. If he gets home before we go to bed, I'll put my wine in a coffee cup and read in our master bedroom. I'll sneak into the kitchen for a refill when he's watching TV. Later, I'll ask if he wants to have a nightcap with me. That's the routine.

I'll put David to bed at eight thirty p.m., and I'll be asleep by nine. Booze, antidepressants, and menopause have tanked my ability to stay awake, as well as my sex drive, though I dismiss the latter as a byproduct of having had so much sex in my life. Maybe I'm just full. I take pride in the fact that I'm not the kind of drunk who slurs her words and falls down. I don't black out. I just check out.

But sitting with the pharmacist, I make the decision to check back in.

I don't want to keep bartering with myself every day for the rest of my life. I'm sick of waking up determined never to drink again, but going to buy booze by late afternoon. I can't keep having stomach issues at inopportune times. Always asking if there's a bathroom nearby.

A few days earlier, I lost control of my bowels in the back of a taxicab in Abu Dhabi. I managed to keep news of the explosion to myself, as David stared out the window at the passing billboards, reading them in Arabic and translating them for me. We'd missed the bus, so I'd hailed the cab to get him to school on time.

When we pulled up at David's school, I eased myself out of the vehicle. I told the driver to wait for me. The only place I needed to go was the restroom.

"Mom, you are walking funny. Are you okay?" David asked.

"Where is the women's bathroom?" I answered calmly.

He pointed. I teetered into the loo. I couldn't find the light switch, so I sat on the toilet in the dark. I wondered how I would clean myself up. If I opened the stall door to let light in, someone might get a glimpse of me. I was very glad Arab restrooms tend to come equipped with a spray nozzle. And because I was wearing trousers and a dress— in an effort to stay covered—I was able to dispose of my pants in the trash can.

I walked out five minutes later as if nothing had happened.

"MOM! WHERE ARE YOUR PANTS?" David screamed.

"I hated them," I whispered. "Go to class now."

Remembering the scene, I decide against taking a cab to work. I can't bear the thought of another backseat blowout. More importantly, I need to talk about what's happened at Burjeel Hospital. And to make a plan for the future—one in which my son doesn't have to question the location of my pants or the status of my liver.

The pharmacist is gone now. It's time for me to leave too.

I send a text to Allan, who is driving the school van today.

Can you come get me?

No cabs at Sky Tower? he responds.

Got RX refill at Burjeel. Need to talk to you.

OK. There in 5 min.

At the beginning of our relationship, Allan and I would watch the sunset with a glass of wine and a plate of Vermont cheese. We'd toast the completion of another day, another of his film projects, another article of mine. The difference was that he could stop at one drink. I always wanted to finish the bottle, and then some.

For eighteen years of marriage, I tried to keep my excesses under the radar. I'd joke about any overt overindulgences.

Honey, I'm a sprinter! I do everything fast! Now give me another glass of that pinot grigio, loser, while you finish your first!

Allan's sole desire is—and has only ever been—to make me happy. But my capacity for happiness is fleeting and finite, like my fast-twitch muscles. Somewhere along the line, drinking became my identity. I want myself back, even though I have no idea who that is.

Moving to the Arabian Desert has stranded me in the farthest reaches of my Sea of Lonely. I tried to blame the excessive heat for my excessive thirst. I tried to blame the region's political climate for churning up my internal conflicts. And I blamed the challenge of obtaining booze for heightening my desire to acquire it.

But all my excuses were quicksand. And even when Allan had offered a rope, I'd thrown it back at him. Noting the escalation in my alcohol intake, and the expansion in my waistline, Allan recently suggested that I consider seeing a nutritionist. I believe my answer was a succinct *"Fuck you!"*

I'd frozen him out of my heart, and our bed, for a few weeks as punishment. I thought about moving far away from him, maybe to Madagascar, with David. Allan brought home flowers and chocolate to make amends. I didn't issue a pardon until a bottle of very expensive champagne was put forth.

Waiting for Allan to drive up, I wonder if God is still willing to help me. I need to find the courage to say the words out loud. *I'm an alcoholic.*

THE EMPTY QUARTER

March 25, 2015

"That's the loneliest place on earth," I told David and Allan as the three of us stared at the big red sun setting into the Empty Quarter—the world's largest contiguous desert. "They call it the Sea of Sand."

We'd driven down to Qasr Al Sarab, an Emirati resort near the border of Saudi Arabia, to celebrate David's birthday, as a family. The previous weekend we'd hosted a bowling party for his school friends at one of Abu Dhabi's huge malls.

Eleven years earlier, David had made his debut at the rural hospital in Harrisonburg, Virginia, where I was coaching. He took forty-eight long, slow hours to come out, after nine difficult months for his thirty-eight-year-old mother. I'd been tempted to write *A distance swimmer was born to a sprinter on March 21, 2004* in the birth announcement.

I'd agonized for a decade about whether or not to even have a child. Fears about keeping a kid alive scared me to death. Headlines about SIDS and childhood leukemia boomeranged around my brain. News of accidents and poisonings intensified the ricochet. Could I put my heart on the line to raise another human being?

Tending to the twenty-one women on my swim team had left me with enough heartache. In the water, they were in control of their thoughts and bodies. But on land, on any given day at least one of them was, like me, in over her head—a parent with a cancer diagnosis, an abusive boyfriend, an unwanted sexual encounter, an eating disorder, substance abuse.

My husband—already the father of two wonderful children—had left the decision about starting a new family to me. I resented the fact that I had to make such a complicated determination for us. But then again, I was glad it was up to me.

Besides, there was the matter of not drinking for nine months. And being a coach had given me reasons to amp up my consumption. I hated the losses and I loved the wins. Either outcome offered an excuse to drink. Meanwhile, I demanded that my swimmers stay dry during the swim season. But my reward for watching them train every day was a bottle of wine every night.

One summer morning, when my swimmers were safely back home with their parents, I decided I was finally ready to be a parent. Having a baby would fill up the hole inside me better than all the booze. In fact, being pregnant would stop me from drinking so much. Becoming a mother was a winning proposition.

I drove the two hours to Washington, DC, where Allan was working on a film.

"I want to have a baby," I told him, undressing in his hotel room.

He laughed, happy to see me and to entertain the idea.

I got pregnant that night, exactly as I predicted and planned—an outcome that stupefied Allan. He later confessed that he thought I'd slept with, and been impregnated by, someone else and that the whole trip to DC had been a ruse to cover my tracks. Had I gone so far as to even reconnect with Bob Kerrey, with whom I'd managed to stay friends since our failed romance? Or was it the James Madison golf coach who looked at me with puppy-dog eyes?

"Jesus, that's fucked up," I told him. "I may be a little crazy, but I'm not pathological."

"I know, sweetheart," Allan answered. "I'm just surprised that I can even make a baby at my age."

He was fifty-eight.

I stopped drinking for the subsequent 274 days. I threw up throughout the first ninety of them—in the trash can on the pool deck at early-morning swim practice, out of the car on the drive home. My pregnancy felt like the longest hangover in the history of the world.

Our trip to Abu Dhabi's stretch of the Empty Quarter in honor of David's birth eleven years earlier was a celebration of our endurance as a family. From our blankets and cushions, after a traditional Bedouin dinner, we had a clear view of the sheltering sky above and the endless desert sand before us.

I wore the long black *abaya* robe that Allan had given me back in December on the occasion of National Day—marking the UAE's forty-third year of independence. My work colleagues had been delighted that I had chosen to don traditional dress in honor of their country. I joked that the country was younger than I was.

I liked the way the abaya fluttered in the wind, moving with me and away from me. Dancing around, like water, even as I stood still. I didn't feel trapped or hidden by the robe, or any less of a woman underneath it. In fact, I felt as free as I ever had in a Speedo.

Our meal was served with one complimentary glass of wine, which I sipped ever so slowly over the five courses. I'd read somewhere that renowned athlete Diana Nyad, who swam the 110 miles from Cuba to Key West at age sixty-four, parceled out M&Ms on flights to make the package last for exactly as long as she was in the air.

Part of me wanted the contents of my one glass to last until the end of time—that I'd never need or want another again in my life. The other part wanted to plead for a whole bottle immediately. I fought to stave off both extremes. Why couldn't I feel or drink in moderation?

I asked the server if we could sleep on our blanket instead of going back to our room—where the contents of a minibar beckoned. Maybe I could go without more for one night if I stayed in the desert.

"The fire will go out, and you may become cold," he responded. "But I will bring you many blankets to keep you warm."

The thought of being cold and sand vipers seeking us out for heat helped me justify going back to our room. We stayed until the fire died out, sitting in silence, letting time pass quietly. I felt no need to measure it or control it. The great emptiness of the Quarter filled me up.

Back in our hotel room, I took a long bath in our huge tub. Then I opened the minibar and took out the two tiny vodka bottles. When Allan and David fell asleep, I reached back in for the Baileys Irish Cream.

THE PERSIAN GULF

March 28, 2015

"It's time," I tell Allan, forcing myself to say it before I can change my mind. Walking out of Burjeel, I decided it was now or never—the same words swim coaches use to psych up a swimmer who's trying to make an important qualifying time.

Allan is pulling out of the parking lot and into Abu Dhabi traffic.

"For what?" he answers, pushing up the lid of his baseball cap. A few strands of white curls poke out around his ears. Allan's hairline has receded in the years we've been together, but what's left still stands straight off his head. He still looks like Einstein and still dresses like a teenage boy in Converse sneakers, snug designer jeans, and rock 'n' roll T-shirts. In Abu Dhabi, he wears a colorful scarf every day to protect his neck from the sun.

I think he's worried about what is going to come out of my mouth. Am I going to announce another pregnancy, even though I'm in menopause and we haven't fucked in months? Might I declare our impending departure for some other far-flung place like Bishkek, Kyrgyzstan?

"Time for me to stop drinking." I drop my head down toward my bloated stomach. I can't look at him. "I'm an alcoholic."

Allan pulls the car over in a Lebanese bakery's parking lot. He turns to give me his full attention. His normally ruddy complexion has gone pale. It's a boiling-hot day in Abu Dhabi, but I feel like I'm dangling off the face of Everest.

"My blood pressure is high. My liver hurts. I'm sick, Allan."

My own words impale me, but I can't cry. Even the water-making machine inside of me is broken. My whole relationship with liquids is broken. I am broken.

I see tears gather in Allan's eyes as he struggles for words. Normally, he'd be chatting up a storm. He loves to tell stories of working with famous film directors. He smiles even when talking about growing up in poverty in Montreal, Quebec. Allan is ebullient when taking out the trash or cleaning the toilet. Upon meeting him for the first time, my father turned to me and said, "How can you stand his constant happiness?"

Now Allan is sad, and speechless. I'm sure he's holding back a "Thank God!" or "Finally!" But he doesn't want me to feel worse than I already do. What could he say?

"Wait here," he finally blurts. "I'll get you a *manakish*."

He goes into the restaurant to buy time as well the traditional Middle Eastern baked dough that we both love.

I send another text to my boss, Ali, about running a little later than anticipated.

No prob, he responds. We have a rock-solid work relationship and friendship, but I'm not going to tell him—or any of my colleagues— what is going on with me. I don't want them to think, even for a second, that I'm some kind of weak heathen. And I don't want to serve as proof that Americans are reckless lushes.

Allan returns with two *za'atar* manakish. We eat them in the car, as if everything is fine. We're just two North Americans in a white van in a parking lot in the Middle East. If the scene were inverted—if we were two Middle Easterners in a white van in a parking lot in North America—we'd be under suspicion.

"Any thoughts on how you'd like to handle this?" Allan says.

"None."

"Help from a professional? Should we try to find an AA meeting somewhere?"

"Wouldn't know who to call or ask. I want to do this my way."

"By yourself?"

"With you."

"Of course."

"Can you take me to work now?"

"Unless you'd rather rest at home. We could go back to Burjeel, check you into a room."

"No. Just get David from school at four thirty and then pick me up at five. I don't want to go home in a cab. I'll obsess about Spinneys."

Allan starts the van and pulls onto Al Muroor Street. We drive the ten minutes to my university in silence.

"I'll cook chicken soup for dinner," Allan offers.

"Let's watch a movie. The three of us. Together. On the couch, with blankets."

"I'll bring a DVD from school," Allan says.

"No James Bond," I request. "Those fucking martinis. How about *Finding Nemo*?"

We both laugh.

Also amusing to me is the image of our family cozied up under blankets on our small couch in Mangrove Place apartments, on Reem Island, in Abu Dhabi, United Arab Emirates—while one of us tries to go without alcohol for the first evening in a long, long time.

"Get *Lawrence of Arabia*," I suggest. "He wasn't a big drinker."

I ran into Peter O'Toole once, in a Tube station in London. I saw those blue eyes in person—inches from my own. I'll never forget the day, which was something straight out of a film. I'd spent the morning in a pub watching coverage of World Cup football because there wasn't a television where I was staying. Due to the early hour, I sipped tea. An elderly man, drinking pint after pint of Old Peculier beer, occupied the neighboring table. We did not acknowledge each other.

Our peaceful coexistence came to a crashing halt when a group of exuberant football fans came in shouting for their team and rounds of beer. They pounded their fists on the table and yelled at the television screens. The old man seemed shattered by the noise and revelry. He pushed his chair back and steadied himself into the standing position. He shuffled in my direction, put his hands down on the table, and leaned over.

"What we need now," he said in a very posh accent, "is a multidirectional splatter button."

I understood exactly what he meant. He wanted to blow the little buggers into bits and pieces.

And now, thousands of miles from London, I've just pushed the multidirectional splatter button on my life.

"You can do this, Nancy," Allan says when we pull up at my school. "I will do everything to help you. Anything."

"Did you know it had gotten this bad?" I ask.

"Yeah," he says.

I grab his hand. We can't hug in public—even in the car. We're parked at the main gate, where students, faculty, and staff are coming and going.

"Should we cancel our trip to the Seychelles this weekend?" he asks.

"No," I answer, although I don't know how I'll fly without alcohol, let alone navigate life on land. "It's your birthday trip. We're going."

Ever since my first transatlantic flight to Africa in 1986, I've relied on Ativan and alcohol to hurtle through time and space. Even under their muting influence, I stared out the window on red alert for any potentially bump-inducing clouds and tried to prepare myself for the impending discomfort.

Did I seek fearful situations because they justified my desire to drink? Did I subconsciously welcome my Sea of Lonely so alcohol could soothe it? Would I even want to travel if I were sober? Would my marriage survive?

"I can do this," I say, although I'm afraid of what the next few days will bring. I've researched, many times, the symptoms of withdrawal. I'm going to feel extremely bad for an extended period of time. I'm going to be extremely angry—about all the things I've been covering up with alcohol as well as the sudden loss of my panacea.

Sometime in the future, though, I will feel better. But that day is a long way away. I reassure myself that I excel at difficult things. Rising up at the end of a race was my signature move in the pool. I can apply it to going sober. I can win this thing too.

"See you at five," I tell Allan.

I get out of the car and walk onto a campus full of people who've most likely never taken a sip of alcohol in their lifetimes. Stepping through the security gate, I put all thoughts of drinking behind me. I smile at the notion that, from this day forward, my relationship with alcohol will exist only in the past. And everything else that happens is my present.

PART II:

AFTER

THE INDIAN OCEAN

April 2, 2015

I'm in two places at once. My body is on the main island of the Seychelles in the middle of the Indian Ocean. But thanks to alcohol withdrawal, my organs feel like they are in the center of Chernobyl's Exclusion Zone.

I'm trying to downplay my symptoms—nausea, crushing fatigue, headaches, weepiness—because this is Allan's seventieth-birthday celebration. I picked the location and booked the trip as a present to him, but I also had some unfinished (more like unstarted) business with the archipelago.

Back in 1986, when I received an acceptance letter from the US Peace Corps, my post was first listed as the Seychelles, where I was to give swimming lessons to children and adults. Like many island nations, the Seychelles has an inordinate number of drowning deaths each year. The people there make their living from the ocean, but also frequently lose their lives to it—often just a few feet from shore. I was thrilled about the assignment and the chance to help people in paradise. I read everything I could find at the library about the tiny country.

When I told my father that I was headed to the Seychelles, he ordered the Berlitz cassette tapes so I could learn French. Two tapes into the set—and able to ask, uselessly, for directions to *le Métro* in Paris—the Peace Corps called, saying that I was headed to South Yemen instead.

Before my dad could order Arabic tapes, the Peace Corps said I was bound for Kenya. There was no time to order the Swahili tapes, because I was on a plane to East Africa soon thereafter. The Peace Corps provided intense in-country language training, and I was nearly fluent after three months, which was music to my father's ears when I told him.

Allan's birthday, and being in Abu Dhabi, provided the perfect opportunity to finally see the Seychelles. While booking the trip four months earlier, images of drinking wine at our oceanfront hotel had danced in my head. The hotel had a minibar and twenty-four-hour room service. I wouldn't have to worry about finding booze in the Christian nation. My husband's birthday would also be a gift to me. I never imagined the gift would mark five days of sobriety instead.

My long-awaited trip was delayed another six hours due to a sandstorm that closed schools, businesses, and roads across Abu Dhabi. Sandstorms, to me, are the most frightening of all weather. The world closes in around you, like vertical quicksand. With enough wind and desert, a person could be buried alive in the upright position.

Huge flat-screen televisions in Abu Dhabi's glistening airport broadcast even-more-terrifying news: terrorists killed 147 college students in Garissa, Kenya. Looking for in-depth coverage on my laptop, I also read the local news that flights from the UAE to the Indian Ocean were being rerouted to avoid dangerous Yemeni airspace.

The sandstorm wasn't the only the thing closing in on Abu Dhabi; regional conflicts were too. Looking closer at a map of the area, I noticed that the Persian Gulf was labeled as the Arabian Gulf. Which was the right name? Had I been referring to the body of water out my apartment window incorrectly? I looked for answers about the discrepancy.

The Gulf has been under dispute for decades, if not centuries. The Persians laid first claim and continue to attach their history to the water. The Arabs, on the other hand, claim it as part of their peninsula. I made the decision to side with the Arabs on the matter—and as a way to mark my transformation in their land.

Shortly before nightfall, during a reprieve in the weather, Air Seychelles departed Abu Dhabi. We landed five hours later at Seychelles International Airport on the island of Mahé. The flight marked the first time in my adult life that I'd flown without being under the influence of alcohol. I was surprised to find that I had less anxiety about turbulence *without* booze in my system. I was beginning to understand that drinking had made everything in my life worse, not better.

I wake up early on Good Friday—the third anniversary of my father's death—to watch the sun rise over the Indian Ocean. The view from our balcony offers views of clear blue skies and water as far as I can see.

While my family continues to sleep, I take stock of my tenuous situation as a newly sober human. I feel slightly reborn, but also heavily wounded. Indeed, everything I feel seems to be in conflict. Carl Jung described the process of redefining yourself as a "tension of opposites," a bridge between consciousness and the unconscious. If I can hold the tension long enough, without succumbing to the urge to identify with one side or the other, then a brand-new self-image will debut. While I stare at the sea, I wonder who I will come to be.

When the sun is up, I put on my swimsuit, the hotel bathrobe, slippers, and my big floppy sun hat. I walk out to the swimming pool and jump in—propping my chin on the pool deck to resume my sea gazing. One of the waiters asks if I want coffee, and I do. Soon I am experiencing a liquid trinity: sitting in a pool, looking at the water, drinking coffee.

But then my stomach churns, and what was inside comes out again. I know that drinking a mimosa would make me feel better in the short run, but I refuse to go that route. It's the long run for this former sprinter from here on out. I have absolute tunnel vision on this matter, the way I always did before a race when I stared at the water I was about to conquer. Whenever the desire to drink comes up, I imagine myself swimming through it. And soon enough I find myself on the other side of longing.

By the time Allan and David wake up, I've had toast and ginger ale. I pretend that I'm fine and dandy, and mostly I am. After they have breakfast, we set out to explore the island in our rental car. Allan says, every hour or so, how proud he is of me. The more he says it, though, the more I realize how bad the situation must have been. I'm tempted to demand silence on the subject, but part of me wants the accolades. My former system of rewards has been shattered. I'm in the market for praise.

The beauty of the Seychelles is hallucinogenic for someone like me, coming from the desert and being newly sober. Color is exploding in every direction. Green palm trees. Red hibiscus flowers. Powder-blue sky. Sparkling-white sand. The sea is the craziest translucent blue-green color that I have ever seen.

I try to ignore the colors coming at me from all directions and concentrate on the narrow two-lane road, which has been carved out of the hills with little room to spare on either side. If I swerve two inches to the left, the left tires will fall into a narrow but deep ravine. If I swerve two inches to the right, I will have a head-on collision with one of the buses carrying people to Good Friday church services.

I want to pull over for an orange Fanta, like I used to in Kenya, but all the little shops are boarded up for the holiday weekend. We had a nice setup at the hotel; there'd been no reason to go looking for more. But that's what we do. We look for more, especially when I'm at the wheel.

We eventually arrive at a beach named Beau Vallon on the other side of the island. The idea that the beach is called "Beau," like my father, is comforting. I see it as a sign that he's cheering me on again. *You can beat this, gal.*

I park the car, and the three of us run into the surf. I buy coconuts from a man who cuts them open and inserts long straws. Walking across the sand with my unwieldy coconut collection, I look like a juggler who's forgotten what to do. The image makes me laugh out loud.

We spend the day on the beach, without towels or chairs. We sit on the edge of a stone wall and swim in the warm, clear water. I feel far removed from the rest of the world. In fact, the Seychelles seems like the farthest I've ever been. But where was the starting point—the center of my universe? The Philippines? Florida? I look at David building a sand castle. The answer is right there: he's where I begin and end.

I don't want to go back to the hotel, where our fellow guests will soon commence with happy hour by the pool. I want to sleep on Beau Vallon until a year from now and wake up on April 3, 2016, with year of sobriety under my belt. How will I get there from here?

I come up with a plan for our return to the hotel—a way to keep my mind off the poolside cocktails and propel me forward in time. We'll borrow masks, snorkels, and fins from the front desk. We'll swim among the brightly colored fish in the shallows. We'll look at them. They'll look at us. Underwater, I can imagine a place—somewhere in this great big sea or perhaps another—where I am completely free and utterly me.

THE ARABIAN GULF

March 28, 2015

After the morning at Burjeel Hospital, I sat in front of my computer at work, almost afraid to move a muscle for fear that I might change my mind about quitting drinking. I updated the university's website with news of a student's first-place win in a drone-making contest. My colleagues strategized about an impending alumni dinner and the need for a guest speaker. They asked me to write a script for the program, which would be translated into Arabic.

I stared at my screen in silence, occasionally glancing over at the one other Westerner in our department. Ali had given the two of us the glass annex so we could write in relative peace while the others hashed out events, contests, and ceremonies in loud Arabic and English. I'd joked with Ali about putting the white girls in a glass house.

"Don't throw stones while you're in there," he laughed.

On the day I decided to quit drinking, I couldn't have thrown a stone if I wanted. I was physically and emotionally exhausted.

"Nancy Ajram," Fareed called out. "What's up?"

I liked that he and the others associated my name with a famous Lebanese pop star. There was no *me versus them* here, the way I'd felt in Korea. I was part of this Bedouin tribe. They were part of me.

"Busy, guys!" I hollered back. "Just tell me when you need the script!"

"Wanna go get ice cream at the Circle K?" Mohammed chimed in.

"I'll pass today, *shukran*."

At high noon, Amir went into the prayer room behind my desk, as he always does. I considered going in with him, even though men and women aren't allowed to pray together. I wouldn't have known what to do, anyway. I just wanted Allah to watch over me in the coming hours, days, weeks. I wanted the same peace Amir received through prayer. He always emerged even more Zen than he already was.

By noon on any other day, I'd have been counting down the hours to my first drink. But on this day, I was counting down the hours to *not* drinking.

Habiba orders lunch for the office every day. We sit together and talk about our work while enjoying food from another region of the Middle East. We've shared a lot of Lebanese meals, in addition to dishes from places like Iraq, Kuwait, and Bahrain.

I'd never been allowed to contribute any money to these lunches. But I always contributed to the conversation. I liked to ask about Habiba's two young children, Fareed's obsession with wandering in shopping malls, Amir's photography, Leila's art studies at the Sorbonne campus on Reem Island, Ali's love for heavy-metal music, and Mohammed's impending military service.

On the day of my decision to quit drinking, I was more of a listener than a talker. But my colleagues wanted to grill me on American foreign policy. Why had the government refused to interfere in Syria? Did my country like seeing Muslims suffer?

"I don't know, guys. I really don't know what my country is collectively thinking. We definitely don't like suffering of any kind. I think

America doesn't know what to do. Kind of a damned if we do, damned if we don't. To save people, we have to kill people."

"We don't mean to put you on the spot," Leila said.

"Here's what I know," I answered. "Being in Abu Dhabi may turn out to be one of the most important things that will ever happen to me. I'll share that with other Americans when I get home. I hope you'll tell people that you knew an American once and she wasn't half-bad."

My colleagues looked at me with such compassion that I thought my heart would burst. Habiba put her hand on my shoulder. I believe Fareed wiped his eye, though he'd never admit to it.

"Habiba, what is that over there by you? It looks burnt," I said, changing the subject to food. "Why didn't we eat that?"

"This?" She pointed to a solid black oval shape near her plate.

"Yeah, what is that?"

"Charred pigeon," she answered. "And it's mine. I'm taking it home for a snack later."

"I definitely won't fight you for it." Habiba was nine months pregnant. The pigeon was all hers. I told her about eating live termites in Kenya and live octopus in Korea. She faked a gag reflex.

Fareed launched into one of his rants about how every culture has bread in common. Food connected us even when ideology divided us. Americans versus Arabs. Christians versus Muslims. Bread was the great equalizer. We could reach across ideology and borders to share it.

"What should the meal be for the alumni dinner?" Ali asked, redirecting us to work matters.

"Bread," Fareed said. We all giggled.

"Nancy, how come you never come to the night events on campus?" Leila asked. "You write the scripts, but you never get to hear them delivered."

Because I'm at home drinking a martini and a bottle of wine, which I won't be doing tonight for the first time in ages. And that's less than three hours from now and I'm freaking out about the war about to erupt inside my body and mind.

"Oh, gotta take care of my kiddo. My husband works late most nights. One day, Leila, I will come. I swear. I mean I promise. I don't swear. Am I allowed to say *swear?*"

"You just said it three times!" Fareed responded, breaking into gales of laughter. The others followed suit. Amir ran to get his camera to get a photo of the mass hysterics and messy table.

"Jesus Christ, you all must think I'm crazy," I managed to say. "Oh no, I said *Jesus Christ.*"

"Twice!" Fareed grinned. Our fits of laugher continued. We grabbed napkins to wipe away the tears.

I watched as Habiba wrapped the fried pigeon in a piece of tinfoil and put it in her purse. I thought more about eating the live termites in Kisumu with Odinga, and the live octopus in Seoul with Jack. I had something in common with those feasts, as well as the Dead Sea. I was still alive and kicking.

THE YAMUNA RIVER

May 14, 2015

A *tuk-tuk* driver is kicking his tires. A small crowd is gathering to examine a dead man whose head is dangling off the curb. A beggar woman is lifting her daughter's disfigured body off their blanket on the ground. An old man is squatting on the sidewalk to release his bowels. Teenage boys in their underwear are soaping up and pouring buckets of water over their heads. Lopsided fruit carts are being pushed into place under shade trees. A dilapidated beauty salon named Glamour is opening for business.

Delhi is greeting the day, just as David and I begin our three-hour journey to Agra to see the Taj Mahal. Our young tour guide, Veer, sits shotgun to our driver and gives an overview of our itinerary while I catch glimpses of the morning's stories starting to unfold. If I'd been hungover, hunched over in the backseat, I would have slept through Delhi's awakening. I haven't had a drink in five weeks, a feat that seems impossible yet all too real, like every scene I'm witnessing outside the car window.

An hour into the trip, we stop for coffee at a rest area along the highway. An Indian mother with her son pauses to snap a picture of David and me eating fresh *idli*—a small savory cake—with our hands from a paper plate. We must look so out of place, despite the fact that we're acting like we belong.

We're seated at the only plastic table that doesn't have an umbrella. Any picture of us will have a terrible glare from the white table. Maybe the woman taking the picture will show it as evidence of ghosts on the Yamuna Expressway between Delhi and Agra.

The Yamuna River running nearby is a tributary of the Ganges, the sacred water of the Hindu people. I wish we had time to see the Ganges, but we don't. The sole purpose of this trip is to see the Taj Mahal and then get back to Abu Dhabi for my work and David's school. Allan is conducting a three-day screenwriting workshop in Dubai, otherwise he would have come with us. Our time in Abu Dhabi is dwindling, so I made a last-minute decision to come to India—a quick and affordable four-hour flight from the Arabian Gulf.

When our van is full of petrol, and we're full from breakfast, we get back on the expressway. David draws in a notepad, but occasionally looks around when I prompt him. He perks up when Veer says something about sugarcane. David asks if he can get some in Agra. Veer's sweet face breaks into a huge grin.

Veer is in his early twenties. He's well educated and speaks Spanish and English. Whenever he gives us facts about India, he repeats the information afterward in verbal bullet points. The technique is effective. Even after all these years and places, and all that alcohol, my brain is retaining more than I thought it could. Being sober is improving my memory. I've stopped waking up every day thinking I have Alzheimer's disease.

We pull into Agra at nine fifteen a.m. to find the city wide awake. The abundance of water buffalo, cattle, and monkeys on the dirt roads forces our driver to swerve and stop in herky-jerky motions. I open my window, hoping the air will ease my motion sickness. I'm hit with the strong smells of fresh flowers and raw sewage, burning incense and funeral pyres.

Five weeks without drinking has lifted a filter from my visual and olfactory lobes. The world is awash in color, stereo, and stench. I vacillate between the desire to take in the sensory assaults and the need to protect myself from them. I roll my window up, only to roll it down again seconds later.

I ask Veer to take us directly to the Taj Mahal before the sun gets too high or too hot. The structure needs to be seen by morning light, as my father told me on several occasions.

"Gal, you've got to take in every detail of Shah Jahan's ode to love before the noontime sun gives the Taj a moiré."

Veer, David, and I enter the sacred grounds from the main gate and see huge crowds in the distance, encircling the Taj Mahal.

"Many people here today," he comments. "More than usual."

We pass through the manicured grounds toward the immense white mausoleum, described as "a teardrop on the face of eternity" by Indian poet Rabindranath Tagore, and "the embodiment of all things pure" by Rudyard Kipling. I can't take my eyes off the Taj as Veer gives us a history lesson. How can something be this beautiful?

"A dream in marble," Veer says, as if he is reading my mind. "Shah Jahan commissioned the Taj in honor of his second wife, Mumtaz Mahal, who died giving birth to their fourteenth child. He wanted his homage to be as rare and beautiful as Mumtaz had been. Built over the course of twenty-two years, at the hands of twenty-two thousand workers, the Taj remains one of the world's greatest architectural wonders."

The structure, to me, looks like grief pointing toward heaven—looking to God for answers about human suffering.

"Mumtaz Mahal's marble tomb rests at the exact center of the inner chamber, enshrined by the Taj, which is perfectly symmetrical and proportional. Hence, the name: Taj Mahal," Veer concludes.

Climbing the stairs to the Taj, we see that most of the people in line are Indians and the line wraps around the entire structure. Veer instructs us not to queue up. I'm reluctant to follow his orders. We should wait our turn too.

But the hundreds and hundreds of people already in line point us in the direction of their destination. They don't want us to wait all day to see whatever it is they've also come to view. They want us to go inside immediately. They seem proud of what is in there. I'm grateful to be given the go-ahead to escape the 111-degree heat. I say thank you to everyone we pass.

Veer tells us what someone else has told him: this is the 350th anniversary of Shah Jahan's death. The lower mausoleum, where he and Mumtaz Mahal are laid to rest, has been opened to visitors. Under normal circumstances, tourists view a replica of the couple's coffins on the main level. Veer says he's never seen the real ones in more than three hundred trips to the Taj.

"You must have a pure heart of love," he says, trying to explain our good fortune. "This is so rare. I can't believe it."

Veer, David, and I descend down a set of narrow stairs to the innermost Taj chamber, which is illuminated only by candlelight. No photographs are permitted. We move, single file, around the tombs. Like I see the others do, I touch Shah Jahan's final resting place and then the one for Mumtaz Mahal. Neither tomb is adorned in any way, in keeping with Muslim tradition. Veer whispers to me that Jahan and Mumtaz were laid facing in the direction of Mecca—not facing each other—to show that only their love of God was greater than their love for each other.

I imagine that I can smell traces of perfume and oils escaping from their coffins. That I can hear faint conversations between them. That I can see, right through the marble, new skin regenerating over their old bones. These two are far from dead and buried. They are alive in anyone who believes in the redeeming power of love.

When we emerge back into the bright sunlight, David and I explore the vast reaches of the structure. I encourage him to absorb the beauty and depth of every tiny nook and cranny. *Look at this inlay of onyx and lapis lazuli*, I say. *Look at the texts from the Quran inscribed around the tall doorways. What do they tell us even though we can't read the script? A story of redemption*, I tell my son.

The sun is so hot, and the humidity so great, that I begin to feel faint, but we have to keep going. We have to commit this place and this moment to memory. In a few days, we'll be back in Abu Dhabi. In a few months, we'll be back in the United States. The Taj will be behind us then. We're right here, right now.

"Are your eyes full?" I ask David when he begins to look overwhelmed and wilted.

He nods. The Taj Mahal is too much to comprehend. After a few hours, you might as well be on LSD. But I'm glad, yet again, to be stone-cold sober. Without a trail of alcohol in my veins, I'm a witness to more than I ever imagined possible.

"Do you understand why I brought you here?" I ask, thinking about my father, who'd been here twice in his lifetime.

"So I could know more about India, and see one of the wonders of the world?" David responds.

"Yes, that's right, but there's one more thing," I say.

"Meet people from India?"

"That too, but there's a larger purpose to this. To all of this."

"What is it?"

"Love always rules, even in death."

THE ARABIAN GULF

March 28, 2015

"The death toll in Yemen's capital continues to rise," Becky Anderson announced on the television. Allan was making chicken soup in the kitchen. David and I were playing Go Fish while I kept an eye on the evening news. Saudi Arabia was continuing air strikes on the Shiite Houthi rebels in Sana'a.

We were trying to act like a normal family, even though nothing was normal. A typical night for us would have entailed a lot of booze for me, a lot of video games for David, and a lot of work for Allan. The usual night for most other American families wouldn't be in Abu Dhabi. And the standard protocol for the first night of going sober usually included tranquilizing medication and medical support.

But I had my own plan for recovery—inspired by the love of my family and my newfound affinity for the surrounding landscape. There's a long history of enduring hardships in these sands; I would simply add mine to the pile.

Besides, I'd terrorized myself in the Middle East and I was hell-bent on saving myself in the same location. Africa had become synonymous with love, and Asia tantamount to death. The Arabian Gulf would go down in my history as the place that changed the course of my life.

By six p.m., though, I was tempted to rescind everything I'd said to Allan in the bakery parking lot. *Maybe it wasn't time. Wouldn't being back in the United States be easier? We'd be home in a few months. Why not wait until then? Just one drink? Maybe tomorrow is better?*

After dropping me at school in the morning, Allan came home to remove every trace of alcohol from our apartment. Thinking of the cupboards he'd emptied, I vacillated between gratitude and rage.

"I can't sit at the dining-room table without wine," I announced when the meal was ready.

"So let's start the movie," Allan said. "Chicken soup with *Lawrence of Arabia*."

David cleared the coffee table and put the movie in the DVD player. I'd told him on the car ride home that I would no longer be drinking alcohol. We'd find things to do together as a family every evening instead of retreating into our rooms with our devices and vices.

"That's good," he'd said flatly. "You liked wine more than me."

I cried all the way back to Mangrove Place and swore never to put alcohol before my child again.

Sitting between the two loves of my life, eating soup and watching Lawrence traverse the sweeping desert, I felt strong enough to stay the course.

When Lawrence extinguished a match between his thumb and forefinger, I took heed of his advice for repeating the gesture.

"The trick," he explained, "is not minding that it hurts."

We stopped the film at nine p.m. for David's bedtime and mine. I tucked him into his cozy bed and Allan tucked me into ours. I stared at the ceiling, wishing I were back on the Bedouin blanket on the edge of the Empty Quarter, as we'd been a week earlier.

I thrashed around. I opened the window to let a breeze into the room. I prayed to Allah, God, Elohim, Brahma, Vishnu, Shiva, Guru.

Why did the world fight over which one should prevail? We needed all of them. I needed all of them.

Three years earlier, on this same date, my father was dying in a Florida hospital bed. He believed in all incarnations of God, but relied most heavily on the one found in the King James Bible.

Dr. Bercaw couldn't speak at the end of his life—a life he'd known would end exactly the way it was ending. His illness had been written in our gene pool and handed down by his father.

I sat with him during his final days. Whenever he opened his eyes, I simply said "Hi!" I couldn't think of what else to utter, what else he'd understand. We just looked at each other. I hoped seeing me was a comfort to him, perhaps breaking through the maze of tangled plaques in his head.

We'd done so much together over the course of our lives, including a dawn ride in a hot-air balloon over the Serengeti Plain, watching the wildebeest migrate across the Maasai Mara in Kenya. Upon landing, we were treated to a champagne breakfast. Because the other people on our safari were nondrinking Muslims from India, my father, stepmother, and I were free to drink all the champagne we wanted. I signaled the server every few minutes to refill my glass.

"We can't waste it!" I said, toasting to our good fortune. I'd consumed a bottle and a half by seven thirty a.m. My father and stepmother enjoyed a few glasses each while zebras grazed just yards from our blanket. My father and I tried to imitate the hyenas' laughing as our driver returned us to Governors' Camp, where I passed out until lunchtime.

Lying in my bed in Abu Dhabi, on my first night without a drink in years, I prayed for forgiveness and for peace. *Father. My father. All fathers. Help me through this night and all the days to come.*

Sweat dripped down my brow. I closed the window and turned up the air-conditioning. I kicked off the covers, only to put them back on again. I opened the window again for air. I counted the number of times I rolled from right to left. I tried to count sheep, but could only get to five. I closed the window. I thought of my father's bravery. I fought against my weaknesses. I imagined myself swimming butterfly, the most difficult and the most powerful of all the strokes, as I headed for dawn.

When Allan came to bed, I asked him to sleep on the couch. I told him that I felt claustrophobic. He kissed my sweaty brow, opened the window, and went back to the living room.

"I love you," he said softly, closing the door. "I'm here."

I calmed myself with the realization that even if I were to go in search of wine or vodka, I wouldn't be able to get any. Spinneys closed at nine p.m. The British Club closed at ten. All the hotel bars and restaurants were shuttered by midnight. Unless I broke into another expat's apartment, there was no way to get a fix.

I repeated *"Allahu Akbar"* over and over again, more than a hundred times, more than a thousand. Then I switched to *"Wahe Guru"* for a thousand more.

Maybe I fell asleep. Maybe I didn't. I lost track of time, but I was awake when the sunrise call to prayer came from the nearest mosque. I watched the sun rise over the canal out my window. The immigrant laborers were in their buses bouncing across the desert. No doubt some of them had endured their daytime plights by drinking the night away. But I knew, beyond a shadow of a doubt, that I would never do so again.

THE RIVER SEINE

June 15, 2015

"More?" I say, pointing my camera toward another café full of wine-sipping Parisians and tourists. Allan gave me the Nikon in Abu Dhabi on the one-month anniversary of quitting drinking. I'm using it now to take pictures of Paris, including the café life that fascinates and repulses me. I can't believe how much people drink.

Abu Dhabi was a good place to go sober after all. Images of booze weren't plastered around town or shown on television. And I easily avoided the hotel restaurants authorized to serve alcohol. Every other establishment in the city was dry. Abu Dhabi was like one big Betty Ford Center compared to Paris.

And France is freezing cold compared to the boiling-hot UAE. We're wearing sweaters and jackets while everyone else is strolling around in short-sleeved shirts, shorts, and skirts. David bought a cable-knit beanie at a souvenir stall on our first day and refuses to take it off, even to sleep.

We're on a five-day stopover in the City of Light on our way back to Vermont. Allan's film school has closed its Abu Dhabi facilities.

David's school year is over. We reached a logical conclusion to our time in the UAE.

Still, I was crushed to leave my work friends. When it was time to say farewell to Ali, I hugged him—even though public displays of affection between men and women were illegal—and burst into tears. Through heaving sobs, I managed to stand before everyone in my office and tell them I would one day walk into their lives all over again. I wasn't able to say what they'd done for me or what I'd accomplished in their midst. But I think they knew some transformation had taken place. After quitting drinking, I'd been more present. I even attended an evening event at the university, where cocktail hour—*for everyone*—consisted of fruit juice in a martini glass.

Crossing the Seine, I find myself regretting the decision to leave Abu Dhabi for a world where people drink in public. The architectural wonder of Paris is littered with billboards advertising alcohol. I'm also surprised by the citizenry's apparel—almost everyone appears half-naked, at least compared to folks in the Middle East. If I'm feeling this uncomfortable and alienated, how do Muslim visitors and émigrés fare when they arrive? The idea that revealing clothing is shocking makes me laugh. I strutted around pool decks in a Speedo for eighteen years, but a year in Abu Dhabi has turned me into a prude.

In Paris, we avoid traditional happy hour—a window of time that continues to vex me—by resting in our hotel room. I can't figure out what to do with myself at five p.m. other than nap. Even though I no longer crave alcohol, I still long for a reward at the end of the day.

Lying in bed with David and Allan reminds me that they are my reward. I rarely let David out of my sight these days. He's my tether and I am his balloon. Without him, I would float away. The Sea of Lonely is now more of a barren desert. I'm walking, like Lawrence of Arabia, toward a place of self-actualization and human understanding. In Abu Dhabi, the Bedouin people were my escorts on the journey. I feel overwhelmed in Paris, like I have to fight against the culture to keep my head above sand.

I'm still finding it difficult to fall asleep at bedtime. I hate the night with the same intensity with which I once longed for it. When the sun has risen, I'm tempted to raise my coffee cup above my head. I am the athlete, the coach, and the audience in this solitary victory that must be won day in and day out. Maybe that's one reason why I keep going instead of turning back. I'm picking up momentum with every second.

After quiet time in the late afternoon, we go in search of a cozy place for dinner—somewhere only a few customers fit inside, which means I don't have to witness lots of people clinking wineglasses and getting animated from alcohol. In the three days that we've been here, I've had escargot and calamari for every dinner, along with a huge bottle of sparkling water. I keep wishing my meals were alive, like the octopus legs in Seoul, so I could fight with them. I feel like a warrior these days, strong and agile. And the fight is my raison d'être.

We wander directionless after dinner, because I'm restless. I feel best in a state of motion. Is this the inevitable outcome of twenty years swimming back and forth in a pool? Am I doomed to a lap-like existence, even without drinking?

Allan finds an old apothecary shop full of little creatures in jars. We spend an hour inside pointing out strange fetuses and organs with great delight. I thumb through old maps. David looks at primitive surgical tools.

"Did you know?" he asks. "That when I lived in your tummy I was literally healing you from the inside out?"

"Where did you hear that?"

"At school. Fetuses produce so many stem cells that they can heal their mother's wounds. Like if you got a cut or something, when I was inside you, it probably healed faster."

I put my arm around him. "You've been healing me every day since then too."

He smiles. "I'm glad you quit drinking, Mom. You seem more real."

I'm so happy with my family in this strange shop that I want to ask the proprietor if we can camp out here for the night—just as I had requested on the Bedouin blanket after dinner at the Empty Quarter.

But this place is more reminiscent of my father's neurology practice, and it comforts me. I'm starting to rejoice in my own odd sensibilities instead of recoiling from them. I do feel more real without alcohol. I'm naked and raw, on display like my grandfather's brain.

Before coming to Paris, I emailed my friend Rick, who's been in the city for two decades. *Could we get together for coffee?* Rick was Jack's oldest friend. They'd taught at ELI in Seoul together, but Rick had left long before I arrived. In fact, he'd married one of his students and they left South Korea and took up residence in New York City for a few years before moving to Paris. We'd first met when Jack and I visited Manhattan after returning to the US. I'd continued to correspond with Rick even after Jack and I broke up.

Rick suggested that our families meet for dinner at a café, and I confirmed with a short note that I no longer drank. Rick didn't know me well enough to be aware that I'd even had a problem—unless Jack had mentioned it—but I still felt like making my status clear. I was reintroducing myself to the world as a nondrinker. I needed practice saying it before getting back to Vermont.

Sitting with Rick, Kyungmee, and their son, Henry, I briefly forget about the existence of alcohol. I delight in hearing about their lives in Paris. Allan and I tell them about our experiences in Abu Dhabi and other Muslim countries. David and Henry converse, too, about school and video games.

The waiter breaks the spell, asking if anyone would like wine. Rick and Kyungmee look at me for approval.

"Of course, go ahead!" I tell them.

"Coffee for me," I tell the waiter. "Bring the pot."

Rick and I discuss the curious case of what I call our "thirty-eighth-parallel lives." He studied English at the University of South Florida, graduating a few years before I did. We never met on campus. His sister lives in Palmyra, Virginia, where my father grew up on a farm. And, mysteriously, we both ended up teaching English at ELI in Seoul, although our paths never crossed there. We were destined to be friends, but time made us wait until we were introduced in New York City.

Rick tells me that Jack lives in Los Angeles now and is doing well in a business with his brothers. I am glad to hear it. I think about how my drinking no doubt contributed to the demise of my relationship with Jack.

We hadn't been able to endure my narcissism—or his, for that matter. In Seoul, Jack's vanity was the perfect fuel for my competitive nature. I wanted to be smarter and more attractive than any girl he'd ever met anywhere. I trained hard for the role, yet Jack never seemed satisfied with my persona or my appearance. Some other girl in his history was thinner or smarter. I took great pride in the notion that I could probably outdrink all of them.

I starved myself down to skin and bones. I even tried to act like Betty Blue, played by Béatrice Dalle in the French movie by the same name, because Jack was so intrigued by her character. I absorbed her persona on top of all the booze I could find.

When I'd reached the zenith of my nadir, Jack no longer interested *me*. By rising up, I'd diminished him. Then, my overt desire to win Jack over turned into a subconscious desire to destroy him. I destroyed much of myself in the process. What a terrible mess, and all in the wake of the terrible circumstances surrounding Carolyn's murder.

Over dessert in Paris, our table of nomads toasts to life. My coffee cup clinks three wineglasses and two Shirley Temples. I feel surprisingly neutral about the booze around me, because of the wonderful people sitting beside me.

THE ARABIAN GULF

March 29, 2015

I glanced down at the floor beside my bed on the first morning of my new sobriety. There was no coffee cup of wine nor any traces of spilled wine or shattered glass. Just the dry floor in all its marble glory. *Thank you, God.*

I got up, steadying myself as if I'd been on a long cruise and didn't yet have my bearings on land. When I was two, our family returned to the United States from the Philippines on a cruise ship. My mother reported one lone side effect of our transpacific crossing: for my first few days back on land I had sea legs, which gave the impression that I was a tipsy toddler.

I took one step from my bed toward the bathroom, testing my steadiness. I slowly walked the rest of the short way and took a good, hard look at myself in the mirror: dark circles under my eyes; a strange pallor to my skin.

I turned on the shower and got in before the water had a chance to warm up. I laughed at the idea of being "dry" and wet at once. I poured shampoo onto my shaky hands and scrubbed my head—the contents run wild, like a herd of wildebeest on the Maasai Mara.

Had anyone in my African past given up drinking? Cemal? Paul? How many teachers from Seoul had sobered up? I'd heard that one particularly heavy drinker from those days had committed suicide in his apartment by sticking his head in the oven.

◆ ◆ ◆

I'd gone back to Seoul in January of 2014—a few months before Allan was approached about working in Abu Dhabi—to put the matter of Carolyn's death to rest in my head once and for all. I spent four days drinking in my old haunts and took a guided tour to the Demilitarized Zone, just as Jack and I had done in the fall of 1988.

I also went to the War Memorial of Korea in Seoul, which opened in 1994. Walking toward the entrance, I heard someone trying to get my attention. I looked around the otherwise-empty courtyard to find an extremely elderly man in a perfectly tailored dark-gray suit on a park bench.

"What country?" he asked.

"USA," I answered.

Twenty-six years earlier, being from the United States wasn't something I would've shouted across a public square. But now, my nationality was met with a huge grin from the old man, as if he'd been waiting all day for an American woman on a secret mission to get right with ghosts in Seoul.

"Help me?" he asked, excitedly.

He waved something in his hand that looked like a checkbook. Did he want me to balance it? I hoped not, because even the most basic math confounded me. I sat down next to him.

He showed me his project—a small diary in which he wrote American phrases in graceful but shaky penmanship. Each English word was translated below in Chinese characters, not Korean.

The first proverb on the page was *Don't fish in troubled waters.* But the old man pointed instead to a lone word next to it in the margin. He then pointed to my mouth, indicating that I should say it out loud.

"MISS-TEAR-E-US," I enunciated.

He carefully wrote out the sound and phrasing in Chinese and then repeated it back to me based on phoneticization. *MS-TIR-EE-US.*

I knew exactly what he was trying to accomplish. During my time in Seoul in 1988 and 1989, I "romanized" key phrases instead of learning to read the Hangul characters of Korea. I wrote down *Me-chu ha-na chu-se-yo* so I could knew how to say "One beer, please" to bartenders. Had I written the Korean characters, I'd have had no idea what to say.

The old man and I continued our efforts with the other words and phrases in his book. *Overtime. Appearance. Don't beat around the bush. Don't be so mean. How kind of you. That's a good idea.*

When all was said and done—a phrase I added to his list—we spoke face to face in rudimentary English and pantomime. He managed to convey that he was a doctor of Chinese medicine and lived nearby the Memorial. Indeed, he was Chinese.

I told him that I was visiting Seoul alone. My husband and son were back in Vermont while I tried to make peace with history. I tried to explain that I'd been holding on to something bad for a long time.

The old man stared at me while I spoke. His eyes narrowed with mine, even if he didn't understand everything I was saying.

"Why did you come to this country?" I asked him.

I couldn't understand his response. He showed me his teeth, which seemed bright and even. I shrugged. But at his urging, I leaned in to get a better look and saw that they were dentures. Was he blaming them for his enunciation troubles?

"Why Korea?" I asked again.

"Japanese. Prisoner."

I remembered hearing that prisoners in Japanese camps during World War II had been subject to brutal torture. Some reported having teeth ripped from their heads with pliers. That's what he'd been trying to tell me—the reason he had dentures.

I leaned my head against the old man's shoulder. We sat like lovers for a while. Standing over us was the *Statue of Brothers*, depicting the quintessential plight of the Korean War: brother fighting against brother for opposing beliefs.

"I wish to see your face again one day," the old man said. I wished the same and let myself cry for the suffering we'd both experienced in Korea.

◆ ◆ ◆

Why had the old Chinese-medicine man come to mind on my first sober day? I toweled myself dry from my long shower and tried to answer my question.

He would have been proud of my decision to take care of myself and to put a war of my own making behind me. I felt a surge of pride too—a feeling rapidly displaced by bile traveling like a train from my stomach to my mouth.

I threw up. I wiped my mouth roughly with the towel as if I were a boxer like Rocky. Suffering was the price of winning. I could endure it.

Coffee. I wanted the brown liquid even though my stomach was in knots. I craved the substance. Had I traded addictions overnight? Had the world flipped? Would I dread the night from now on and the time at which I used to drink alcohol? Would I, instead, find myself praying for the dawn and the appointed time to flood my bloodstream with caffeine?

I put on my flower-print bathrobe and walked into the hallway. I opened David's door to look at my sweet sleeping son. I crawled in bed next to him and wrapped my arms around him.

"Good morning, Mommy," he said, sweetly.

"*Great* morning, little D. I love you to the ends of the Earth."

"Can I sleep a few more minutes?"

"Yes." I went to the kitchen where Allan was making toast and coffee. I put my arms around his waist.

He kissed my head.

"I've never been more proud of you," he said.

"I feel incredible and horrible," I responded. "On a more practical note, I don't think David has a clean school uniform to wear today."

"He can wear the one from yesterday," Allan answered. "Are you going to work?"

"I can't make a decision. About anything. Where should I drink my first cup of coffee? In the living room or in our bed, where I used to drink wine? Should I reclaim that space? I really don't know how to proceed with anything."

"You could go swim in the Persian Gulf at the British Club."

"Allan, it's the Arabian Gulf."

"Right."

"And, just so we're clear, any reference to my drinking days is in the past tense now."

"Got it," he answered. "So what about going for a swim at the club?"

"The servers will bring me wine like they always do."

"Tell them no thanks."

"I'll be saying it for the rest of my life. I guess I could use the practice."

Practice. I'd had none for *this* day. I had no idea how to proceed. How would I walk out of this apartment and into the world as a nondrinker? I'd walked into so many places in the world, but rarely stonecold sober.

"Maybe I will stay home and watch the rest of *Lawrence*. That scene where he arrives at Sinai and the guy on the motorcycle screams, 'Who are you?'"

"You should give thinking a rest," Allan said. "Let it be."

"I don't know how to do that."

Allan handed me a cup of coffee. I sat on our couch and turned on the TV.

"Potential for rainstorms in Abu Dhabi this afternoon," said the Sky News weather reporter. "Drivers should use extra caution. The unstable weather pattern could extend into tomorrow."

I hadn't seen rain since arriving in Abu Dhabi eight months earlier. In Kenya, rain was my favorite part of every day. I'd stand in my back doorway and gaze out at the Maragoli hills, thinking of Lake Victoria behind them. Rain in Abu Dhabi felt like a promise of good things to come.

"Promise me we'll go to Kenya one day," I called out to Allan.

"I promise," he answered from the kitchen. "We'll be nearby on Friday, you know. The Seychelles!"

"Right." I'd almost forgotten. "I should definitely swim today, in the Arabian Gulf, even in the rain. Get myself ready for the Indian Ocean."

THE ARABIAN GULF

April 17, 2015

Three weeks into sobriety found me in a Speedo, ready for the swim portion of the Five Star Aquathlon on the grounds of the Emirates Palace hotel. The word *aquathlon* made me laugh every time I said it. Why not aqua-thon? Was the *l* really necessary? And why did it have five stars? Everything in Abu Dhabi was high class, even a five-hundred-meter swim and two-kilometer run.

I'd signed up for the event on my very first sober day, after taking a short swim at the British Club and reading about the "Aquathlon" on a poster in the locker room. I needed something to fixate on other than the loss of booze. I wanted a goal, a trophy for my efforts, and swimming in a competition all but guaranteed one.

The trophies lined up on the officials' table at the event were magnificent glass structures intended for the top three places in each category. At age forty-nine, I fell into the masters' group. I figured I could outswim anyone in the water, especially in this age category, even though I hadn't trained in years. The run would be a different story. I'd have to try to hold on to any lead I earned in the water.

Stave off the encroaching competition, as I'd done so well in the pools of my youth.

But I wasn't an athlete anymore. I was a recovering alcoholic. I was pudgy and clumsy. My head was foggy from sleepless nights, which had tortured me since day one of sobriety. Like an infant, I was learning how to put myself to sleep without a bottle.

When I felt most challenged by difficult days and nights, I pretended that I was about to swim two lengths of a pool in 23.69 seconds. I narrowed my eyes and looked down an imaginary lane, staring so intently that I lost sight of the periphery. I tried to see myself winning, arms raised high at the finish line. The Five Star Aquathlon offered an actual race after weeks of imagining myself in one.

Allan had school business in Dubai, so I brought David along with me, at the crack of dawn, for the big event. I'd realized a few days beforehand that I'd need someone to keep him company while I competed. The days of leaving him alone with strangers were over.

I found that person on Facebook in the form of an old Peace Corps friend from Kenya who'd recently moved to Abu Dhabi for work. I'd seen Larry one other time since then, in Seoul, right after Carolyn's murder. He'd just happened to be in South Korea and found me through friends. When I emailed him out of the blue, Larry said he was happy to come along to the Aquathlon.

David, Larry, and I walked around the impressive Emirates Palace grounds for a little while to get our bearings. It was known as one of the world's few seven-star hotels, and the cost for staying in the Palace could be thousands per night. The race was set for a little stretch of beach in the hotel's private lagoon off the Gulf.

Like me, Larry couldn't stop saying "Aquathlon." We doubled over in laughter at the awkward way it made our tongues flop around. David was pretty sure the grown-ups around him had lost their minds. Being with Larry made me feel like a twenty-year-old again.

I asked David if he'd hand me a bottle of water as I passed through the transition area from the water to the run.

"Scream words of support too," I requested. "I'll need it."

"I will, and I'll take pictures," he answered.

"Don't," I said, fearful that my body still looked like shit, even though I'd lost a few pounds.

The officials called all competitors to the waterfront for the start. I lowered my blue goggles to cover my eyes. David took my jogging pants to the transition area so I could pull them over my swimsuit when the time came to run. In the States, I would have done the run in my Speedo. But in Abu Dhabi, I needed to maintain some level of decorum. Besides, I wanted to cover my still-jiggly belly and thighs as soon as I got out of the water.

The competitors gathering around me wore all sorts of stylish gear and outfits and had very lean, athletic bodies. I felt way out of my league. But I wasn't. The water was my home, wherever I happened to be.

With the sound of the buzzer, our mixed-gender group of a hundred or so ran into the lagoon at full speed. I hung back to ensure that I'd have room to swim long strokes and pass the group on the outside. About two hundred meters in, I was at the front of the pack with two others. I decided to maintain the same pace rather than sprint to the lead. I needed to conserve some energy for the run.

I told myself that I didn't have to do the run. I could walk out of the water and sit down on the beach and say "Aquathlon" with Larry and David for the rest of the morning.

With my head underwater, I watched as little fish scattered. I mouthed an apology to them for the disturbance. I kept my strokes steady and long. I kept my breathing calm. The race was only five hundred meters and I could finish it in my sleep, even though I hadn't trained in ages. Swimming to me was like breathing for other people. Instinctive. Natural. Nourishing.

I almost swam right up onto the beach, putting my feet on the sandy bottom when only six inches of water remained. I walked out of the water to the sounds of a screaming crowd.

"Oh my God," Larry yelled. "You're an amazing swimmer!"

I wanted to laugh, but I was panting to the point of not being able to speak. The water had tired me far more than I'd expected. I again considered not doing the run, but my legs just kept going on autopilot.

David handed me the water as I'd asked him. I pulled on my jogging pants and slipped on my sneakers. Compared to the smart-looking competition, I looked like a candidate for hobo school. I laughed despite my heavy breathing. The swim had taken more out of me than I'd expected.

"Go Mommy!" David said. Larry joined him, saying "Mommy" too. *Go, Mommy, go. Go, Mommy, go.*

I could almost hear my dad chiming in with *"Go, gal, go."*

As expected, the pack started passing me on the run. I managed to stave off one woman who seemed to be about my age, as we rounded the corner to the finish line. I saw the table of trophies reflecting the sunlight. I wanted one with as much conviction as the bronze masterpiece I'd coveted back at my swim club in Florida when I was eleven.

I sprinted to the finish line, passing another woman at the end. I completed the race in less than thirty minutes, better than expected. A volunteer hung a large medal around my neck, just for finishing.

Larry and David hugged me tight, even though I was having trouble catching my breath. My face was hot and red. I ran back into the water to cool off.

I pounded my fists on the water with joy as if I were Michael Phelps in the Olympics.

I did it.

A short while later, an announcer called out the awards in the women's masters division.

"In third place," he said, "Nancy Bercaw!"

I walked up to the podium, soaking wet in my swimsuit and track pants, and accepted the elegant trophy. I lifted it up, the award signifying so much more than my place in the race. I'd regained my place in the world.

AL JAZIRA NATATORIUM

June 2, 2015

I regained my footing in my office after nearly slipping on a sea of papers scattered across the marble floor.

"What happened?" I asked Ali. I'd come in early to get a start on the day. He'd arrived well before me, for some reason.

"Bring these home," he said, handing me two notepads emblazoned with the university logo. He'd made a mess while searching for a gift to give me. He seemed to feel awkward about both.

As I took them from his hands, I noticed that mine were no longer shaking after nine weeks of sobriety. And they weren't swollen. My wedding band sat comfortably on my ring finger.

A short while later, the special assistant to the university president showed up at my desk. She was American too, and an athlete.

"I just heard that you're a swimmer," she said. "Olympics or something."

"Was," I laughed. "Qualified for Olympic Trials, but didn't go."

"A group of us are helping teach female students here how to swim. Would you be interested in that? I know you are going back to the States soon, but maybe you can be part of one lesson before you go."

"Sure. When and where?"

"At the Al Jazira Club, Wednesday night. From eight to ten o'clock."

"That late at night?"

I loved the idea of helping, but I wasn't used to doing anything during the evening hours, when I was still very much occupied with trying *not* to drown myself from the inside out. I figured that being in the water during those hours, surrounded by a swathe of women who don't drink, would help. Perhaps I needed them as much as they needed me.

"That's open-swim time for females," she said. "It's only offered twice a day, and the other is during class time."

"What's the skill level?"

"All over the map. Some can't swim at all. Some can do a few laps and have fairly good strokes."

"I'd be happy to work with them," I said, even though the idea caused me some anxiety. Did I still know how to coach? Could I teach in a different culture?

My colleague leaned down to whisper something in my ear.

"Some wear full Muslim swimming costumes. Head to ankle. The problem is it weighs them down, but there's nothing we can do about it."

I wasn't interested in altering their swimsuits or their culture, only their relationship with the water. They needed to be able to save themselves in a water-related crisis. Those occasions—boating accidents, falling into pools—rarely come with opportunities to ask someone if it is okay to put on a Speedo before tanking.

My sole concern was how to convey basic stroke techniques to non-native English speakers. The vocabulary of swimming—leverage, rotation, and reach—is very specific. But since classes at my engineering university were conducted in English, I could probably translate physics concepts to stroke technique without too much trouble.

In the cab to Al Jazira Stadium, I wasn't tempted to ask the driver to stop at Spinneys. I focused on the road and the work ahead at the pool. I wanted the lesson to be fun for the girls, as well as informative. I wanted to connect with them, not just coach them. Getting out of my head, if only for a few hours, would be a bonus.

The driver dropped me at the pool entrance, parked his car, and walked to the Bangladeshi coffee shop where a number of cabbies on break had gathered. I opened the Club's side door to locate my tribe.

Al Jazira Natatorium was home to an impressive Olympic-sized fifty-meter pool. I flashed back to a strange email I'd received from my father a few years before he was diagnosed with Alzheimer's. There was no message, per se, only a word he'd "found" in his own mind and his attendant definition.

Nan-a-tor-ium: place where Gal swims.

His email had delighted and frightened me, as did my first sight of Al Jazira Natatorium. I was worried that our novice swimmers would get overwhelmed in the Olympic-sized pool. I hoped the coaching staff had already established a safe lesson protocol. If not, I'd take the lead in these efforts. After seeing the aftermath of that boy's drowning on our short trip to Indonesia, I wasn't about to let it happen to another person in my vicinity. We'd have rescue devices standing by at all times.

One of the coaches was a professor at my university. She greeted me with a handshake. Her physique—broad shoulders, slender hips, long legs—identified her as a former racer. A sprinter, in fact, just like me. I felt a surge of adrenaline, as if we'd come to compete, not teach.

"You must be Nancy," she said with a slight Slavic accent.

She introduced herself as a onetime member of the national team of Yugoslavia/Bosnia in the 50-meter freestyle. She'd trained at the

University of Miami in Florida in the summers. We tried to determine if our paths had ever crossed, but she was ten years younger than I.

The other coaches—a librarian and the president's chief of staff— joined us on deck as our swimmers began streaming out of the women's locker room. Most of them wore swimsuits made especially for Muslim women. A few wore light pants and T-shirts. One actually marched out in a bikini top with denim shorts. A few of them wore swim caps and the rest let their hair hang free or pulled back in a ponytail.

The Bosnian coach suggested that I take the best swimmers to the deep end and work with them while she helped the beginners in the shallow end with the other coaches.

I asked my team, as I called my eight apprentices, to dangle their legs in the water while I gave a short demonstration of the techniques we'd cover. The most important of which, I said, was getting back to the pool wall when fatigued.

"Never, ever stop kicking," I said. "The muscles in your legs are the largest, and they will carry you back no matter how tired you get."

I asked the group to swim out to me, about ten feet from where they'd been sitting. We all treaded water for a minute before I instructed them to swim the crawl to the wall.

"Swim slow and steady," I advised. "There is no need to sprint. Make your strokes even and purposeful. Hold on to the water as if it were a solid mass. Don't let it slip through your hands."

Survival over speed was a new concept for me as well. I swam along with them, letting most of the girls finish before me.

I asked them, from their positions holding on to the wall, to pull themselves onto the deck, using only their upper-body strength.

"First, try it with your arms set wide apart."

They struggled to pull themselves up the twelve inches from water to deck. Arms collapsing in the process, sending them back in the water.

"Now try it with arms and hands at shoulder width."

I demonstrated, transporting myself from water to land with one motion. The women followed suit.

"Why does that work better?" I asked.

"Physics," one answered. "Fulcrum, load, effort."

"Na'am," I said. *Yes* in Arabic. "Let's talk about that in terms of stroke efficiency. If your arms are wide under your body when swimming, you won't have as much leverage on it."

I demonstrated while standing on deck. *Arm reaches out in front. Pulls down through the water under the body. Recovers with bent elbow though the air.*

As they practiced on land, I corrected their form. I instructed them to jump in and re-create the movement in the water.

"Yallah," I said. *Let's go* in Arabic. A few of the women chuckled at my poor pronunciation.

We completed the evening lesson with a game of Sharks and Minnows. I was the shark who tried to tag the minnows as they made their way from one side of the pool to the other. To escape me, they had to kick hard and pull efficiently and get to the wall.

Exhausted by the effort, we all sat on the deck to recover. Some of the women were laughing from the fun and infected the rest with the giggles. I found myself in hysterics before long too. When I finally looked at the clock, I saw that it was ten p.m. I'd gone two nighttime hours without thinking about alcohol.

WINOOSKI PUBLIC POOL

June 23, 2015

I grew up swimming near the Gulf of Mexico before making my way across the Seven Seas as a drinker. I gave up drinking on an island between the Arabian Desert and the Arabian Gulf. And now I find myself stone-cold sober on a swimming-pool deck in Vermont.

I marvel at my trajectory, but I'm even more excited by the sight of my son walking to the starting blocks to swim his first race ever: the 50-yard freestyle.

The public-pool facility in Winooski, a town adjacent to the city of Burlington, is alive with swimmers and parents. Green ribbons will be handed out to heat winners. There's no high-point award for each age group. I chew on my bottom lip, worrying about my son's entry into this treacherous world. What would be his reward for enduring it?

David's first swim lesson took place when he was two at the Burlington YMCA. I pointed out the big kids doing swim practice when his lesson was done.

"Wanna be on the team one day?" I asked.

"No! No racing, Mommy!"

He repeated the same vow every year as he moved through the program's ranks at a snail's pace. *No racing, Mom!*

In Abu Dhabi, David continued his tortoise-like progress with the Gulf Star Sports swim school and vehemently maintained his noncompetitive oath.

"*Laa*, Mama!" he'd said in Arabic. *No!*

But just as we were about to leave the country, David had a sudden change of heart. He asked to join the swim team as soon as we returned home to Vermont. The instant the words emerged from his mouth, I logged on to the YMCA's website.

"*Boom!* You're in, kid," I said, restraining my urge to dance a jig. I'd been sober for a while, and I'd latched on to the idea that the loss of my addiction could become my greatest victory. I wasn't letting go. The thought of David on the swim team was added glory.

During the first week of practices, I watched David do poolside exercises like I'd done in my days. He did ten sit-ups and ten push-ups. He was unsteady on the slippery deck, which is the whole point of "dryland" training—swimmers learning to grapple with the forces of gravity outside their preferred element. It's a lesson to be tucked away for later. In my case, a full thirty years later.

I watched David swim every single lap too and was taken aback by his endurance. He managed to continue even when he appeared fatigued. He never sped up; he never slowed down. He never faltered.

He did crash into the lane line and into the other swimmers a half dozen times, but quickly shrugged it off. He practiced diving from the starting blocks, which resulted mostly in belly flops. Yet he never complained. His swim team trained during what was still my most difficult period of the day, between five and seven p.m. I was grateful for the distraction. The hours I spent watching him swim soon became the happiest of my day.

As he steps on the block for his very first race ever, David has a little smile on his face. I wipe away a tear. I shift my focus to the boy in my lane, because I've volunteered to be a timer. Allan is doing the same thing for the kid on the other side of David.

During our timers' meeting before the meet, we'd been given instructions for operating a stopwatch. I pretended I was new to the game. I didn't want to tell the group how I'd lived and died by the god-damned things for twenty years. I wanted to be a mom, not a former swim champion or recovering alcoholic.

"Swimmers, take your mark," the starter says. I watch as David bends down and holds the front of the block. My shoulders tighten.

With a loud beep, the boys are off. David's strokes are even and steady. He stays in the center of the lane. He manages to do a flip turn. He maintains his pace all the way back toward the finish. He's behind the others by about two body lengths. David appears to complete the race in a little over a minute.

I watch my son shake hands with the racers on either side of him. He gets out of the water with the biggest grin I've ever seen on his face. I run over and hug him with the biggest grin I've ever had on mine, as does Allan.

David goes on to swim the 50-yard breaststroke but gets disqualified for turning over onto his back at the wall. I'm tempted to yell at the official, but his call is the reality of this sport. Rules matter, even for beginners. Besides, David doesn't care about winning or being disqualified. He likes swimming for fun.

I proceed to shed a few more tears thinking about my sweet mom, still living in Florida, who spent so many years of her life taking me to morning and afternoon workouts and swim meets across the state and country, while my father worked. I was never grateful enough for her sacrifices. I'd find a way to make up for it.

I put my sunglasses over my eyes as I continue crying in memory of my father, who remembered every single one of my times and records until Alzheimer's disease stole every single memory from him. Here I stand now, committing my child's very first race times to memory and praying these recollections endure. *Insha'Allah. God willing.*

"I am so proud of you. So proud of you," I tell David. I almost can't stop saying it, as if I'm addicted to the words. I sound like Allan did when I first quit drinking. He expressed his pride every second he could, and still does. I get flowers once a week.

David shrugs off my praise and makes his way to the snack bar. I hand my watch to a substitute timer and go with him.

I take money out of my wallet, which includes six quarters and one rupee. I show the foreign currency to David.

"A month ago we were in India," I say. "Weird, huh?"

"Not really," he laughs. "Airplanes are quick."

"Next time we go anywhere, let's go by boat," I respond. "Slow the journey down. Life goes too fast anyway."

I am glad we're in the here and now. My drinking days are behind me; David's swimming career is just beginning. We both have traction on things that almost never came to be.

THE ARABIAN GULF

June 14, 2015

When the time came to say good-bye to Abu Dhabi, I feared our farewell party more than I dreaded our actual departure. We'd invited a small circle of friends to join us on a two-hour sunset cocktail cruise through the canals leading to the Arabian Gulf. The very waterways I'd stared at—drunk, hungover, and sober—from my bed in Mangrove Place.

On the appointed evening, the staff at the British Club loaded up the *Luluwa Dhow* with drinks and hors d'oeuvres. I made sure sparkling water was on the menu as well as calamari.

The British Club was permitted to serve alcohol anywhere on its waterfront property and its seafaring vessels. President Sheikh Zayed bin Sultan Al Nahyan, who recognized the need for Europeans in helping him build the Emirates, donated the Club's land to a group of enterprising expats in the early sixties. Those ranks had since grown to nearly four thousand members from all over the world.

Before I quit drinking, I loved to sit in the shallow beach waters in the evening while sipping wine from a big plastic cup. After I quit, I'd only visit the Club for breakfast and swims.

Drunk or sober, though, I resented the fact that poor Indian, Pakistani, Nepalese, and Filipino laborers suffered at some of the club members' command.

Bring me another beer, Ali, and be quick about it, for God's sake! This steak is overcooked, boy! You're an idiot! That's the wrong receipt, you fool! Why can't you people learn anything?

To be fair, the vast majority of members were exceptionally kind and generous to the staff. At the holidays, we collected money for plane tickets and gifts. Still, I struggled with the feeling that we got more than we gave. I knew that the staff made deeper sacrifices than we could ever imagine or repay.

An hour before our dhow cruise, I wished for the chance to cancel the whole event. I'd be the only nondrinker on board, except for our two Muslim waiters and the children.

I took comfort in the fact that our closest friends in Abu Dhabi had been supportive of my decision to quit drinking. I'd let the news spill out slowly, over a period of weeks—finding it difficult to utter the word *alcoholic* to myself, let alone to anyone else. I'd been so deft at hiding the amount that I actually consumed, people were surprised by my revelation.

Shortly before quitting, I did confide in my best pal Simi about my tendency to go overboard.

"Listen to your heart, Nance," she said over the phone.

"Or my gut," I joked, "which is hanging over my pants in rolls."

We both laughed.

"I'm serious, though, Nance," she continued. "You don't have to continue down any path you don't like. Nothing is written."

"Are all Indian women such wise sages?"

"Just the ones who love their friends," she answered.

Simi had seen me throw back the vodka and the wine during parties at her house in Al Ain. But my boozing had been no more pronounced than that of any other expat guests. Heavy drinking just seemed the logical outcome for people who relocated to nearly inhabitable climates. I suspected that people in Iceland went to similar extremes.

Simi, meanwhile, was the embodiment of moderation. She and her husband Chris were attentive parents to their three children and good stewards of their family's health. When I woke up hungover at their home, Simi made curative Indian tea for me—without judgment or comment.

I was glad she, Chris, and the kids were driving the hour and a half from Al Ain to come on the sunset cruise.

My strategy was to focus on the boat's forward trajectory through the water as a metaphor for my own journey to a better place.

I whispered my plan to Simi when she came on board with her family.

"Perfect," she said. "Unless the boat goes into reverse!"

We shrieked with laughter, and I embraced her with every bit of love in my being. Simi had mentioned early in our friendship that she always limited herself to two drinks to prevent a raging migraine the next morning. I'd responded by saying that I always had more, regardless of the consequence.

But through a miracle of divine grace—and swimmer's determination—I was getting on a seafaring vessel without my addiction along for the ride. I had real traction on a life without alcohol; I wasn't going to go backward no matter what the boat did.

Simi stood by my side for the two-hour ride. She didn't pepper me with questions about how I was holding up. Instead, she held me up with her love.

The dhow cruised slowly ahead. Our guests enjoyed the service and the beverages. I spoke with everyone while keeping one eye on the horizon. I asked our servers to take a break too and enjoy the view. As dusk fell, we heard the calls to prayer rise up from the city. *Allahu Akbar.*

God is great, I repeated to myself. God is great.

LAKE CHAMPLAIN

August 2, 2015

When people in Vermont ask about Abu Dhabi, I tell them that it's the opposite of a Green Mountain existence. But I don't tell them how much I like extremes, because most people don't. I've been going to one end of a pool—or overseas location—and coming back again for my whole life. Perhaps my existence should be characterized as a series of laps instead of years.

Yet I am quick to tell people that Abu Dhabi saved my life. A country of nondrinkers exposed the depths of my addiction to alcohol. I used the call to prayer as a call to change. I want them to hear a different story of the Muslim world than the one shown on their television sets.

I work at the University of Vermont in the Larner College of Medicine as a communications specialist for the Vermont Center on Behavior and Health. My colleagues are researching ways to curb addictions to opioids, tobacco, and food through behavioral incentives. My job is to share their work with the world. The research team doesn't know my story. I'm a former addict working to help addicts. I never saw that coming, yet here I am.

I get up every morning at four o'clock to write for three hours before David and Allan wake up. I once feared that quitting drinking meant I'd have to quit writing too. But I'm writing more than ever, and with more honesty and clarity. The pages add up faster as my drinking days get further away. Words are my water now.

Cemal found me on Facebook, and we're virtual "friends" after a thirty-year absence. He explained, via instant message, how he'd moved back to Turkey after spending a few years in Tanzania. He'd gotten married and had two kids. They were grown, and he'd returned, divorced, to East Africa, where he was back in the food business. At the end of our online conversation, Cemal said that he'd never forgotten me and that he'd never had anything again like what we had that week. He also clarified that he meant no disrespect to my life since and my husband.

I follow the pictures he posts of Kenya on Facebook, but I don't long to be in them with him. Allan and David are my team. I'm at my best when we're together—on the ground, in an airplane, in the water.

David continues to make progress in the pool. He doesn't seem poised to become a champion swimmer, which comes as a relief to me. He won't grow up fighting against everything and everyone. Perhaps he'll glide between destinations and relationships—living between the lines instead of jumping back and forth over them.

One evening, while David is practicing, I get in the pool with the masters team—a small group of former swimmers around my age. The water feels foreign to me. I can't hold on to it as I once did, the way I'd instructed my swimmers at the Al Jazira pool. But I keep going—that's the name of the game now.

Halfway through the workout, smack-dab in the middle of the YMCA's twenty-five-yard pool, I arrive at what feels like a remarkable conclusion: I'm living proof that Hans Christian Andersen's 1836 story about a sea creature sacrificing her tail fin to walk among mortals is a cautionary tale, if not a real one. My father had read "The Little

Mermaid" to me a number of times in my early childhood, on the couch in our fishbowl living room.

Walking away from the pool at the University of South Florida in 1986 had felt like daggers in my soul—not the soles of my feet, as was the Little Mermaid's fate. I'd put thousands of hours into the water, from ages two to twenty, and had no idea how to be a land mammal. Indeed, I had no idea how to be, let alone walk in a new direction altogether.

My identity changed with each new landscape. I felt especially rocky in the arid hills of East Africa, where I taught English as a Peace Corps volunteer. Missing the water, and the strength it had given me, I started pouring copious amounts of fluid inside my gills.

Taking up residence on the Korean Peninsula a year later literally put an even deeper divide between the old me and the new me. I'd moved to Seoul to teach English and to see the 1988 Olympic swimming events in person. For many months afterward, I drowned my sorrows at local bars with soldiers on leave from the DMZ. And then came Carolyn's death, which left a permanent rift in me, almost as deep as the one smack-dab in the middle of the Korean Peninsula.

But it wasn't until I reached the desert sands of Abu Dhabi in 2014 that I saw what drinking overseas was doing to me. Nearly three decades of alcohol abuse had turned my lean frame into an amorphous mass. My blood pressure had gone from a healthy 110/60 to a dangerous 155/99. I was killing myself.

Sober now, and back in the pool, I am whole again. No more fighting gravity, or my demons. As Andersen's story goes, my very survival depends upon being in the water—not just my identity.

THE NORTH
ATLANTIC OCEAN

November 23, 2015

Iceland's contradictory landscape of volcanoes and glaciers stretches out as far as the eye can see, just like the Empty Quarter. The days stretch out for me too, since I'm no longer in a rush to arrive at five o'clock. I seem to have all the time in the world.

We're staying in an Ikea-styled one-bedroom apartment-hotel near the old port and the downtown shops, where we stroll and buy goofy souvenirs. I had to stop myself from buying a T-shirt that said *I had sex with an elf in Iceland*, although it made me laugh like a crazy person. We turn on the TV in the evenings to see what people are watching in this part of the world.

The very first show we see is a Hallmark movie called *Moonlight and Mistletoe*, costarring my husband. The three of us jump around the room as if we'd won the lottery. I high-five Allan in midair. As our hands collide, I'm grateful that our lives collided in a pub in Vermont nineteen years earlier. I'm amazed that our marriage has endured so many hardships, outlasting time and place and addiction. Allan is seventy and I'm a month away from turning fifty. There's no way I could have done this with anyone else, though sex with an Icelandic elf did sound like fun.

Iceland is quirky about carnal desires and sexual organs, as evidenced by the Icelandic Phallological Museum—Reykjavik's penis museum, where we'd spent our first afternoon in the city. Allan and David cringed at the sight of a whale's "Moby-sized" dick in a giant glass jar. I was captivated by the octopus phallus, which doubles as one of the creature's eight arms, according to the sign. Had I inadvertently consumed an uncooked octopus dick in Seoul? My past makes me smile these days, not cringe. Like the octopus in these jars, I am more than my bits and pieces.

During mating, the penis detaches—a defense mechanism as well as mating style—because hungry females are capable of cannibalizing their mates. While she swims around solo, with a penis inside her, a new penis begins the process of regeneration on her lover.

I asked David if he wanted a souvenir from the museum.

"Mom, I want to get out of here!" he yelled, stalking off to find a chair. "I don't want anyone to know I was here."

I lingered amongst the penis collection for a while longer, glad that sobriety had returned my sex drive. I warned Allan to guard his penis because I might be tempted to cut if off and swim around with it inside my body. He winced, and we held hands through the rest of the exhibit.

On our last day in Reykjavik, we take the Golden Circle bus tour to see the top tourist destinations. The first stop is Geysir, where we watch scalding-hot water erupt from the geothermic Earth every few minutes. The blast manages to startle me every time it blows. I can't seem to get used to the inevitable. Meanwhile, the skies can't decide whether to drop snow or rain on us. The heavy clouds give half their efforts to one and then the other.

Back in the bus, we head to Gullfoss Waterfall. I notice that the passenger across from me is slumped over in his seat, clearly hungover. He's snoring and reeks of booze. I am so grateful not to be him that I bounce up and down in my seat like a little kid.

At Gullfoss, we walk to the bottom of the falls and then up to the top—getting two perspectives on the descending water. I can't discern the exact spot where "going down" becomes "coming down." Is there one?

We load back into the bus for our final stop, Þingvellir National Park. Our tour guide explains the historic significance of the site as the home of the first Icelandic parliament. He seems to say something about a "pool for drowning women."

"Allan, is he saying 'pool for drowning women'?"

"I think so. But I can't tell for sure. Why would he be saying that?"

"And if he is saying it, where does the inflection fall? Is this pool for women to drown other people or for drowning the women themselves?"

"What about the men?" David interrupts. "Where do they drown?"

The three of us are laughing again. Loud enough to wake the man who's feeling rough after a night on the town. When he shoots us a dirty look, I stick my tongue out at him. He falls back asleep.

At Þingvellir, we walk a two-kilometer stretch of icy land past a few small pools of water. One of them may be the infamous "pool for drowning women," but we aren't sure.

I run ahead to catch our tour guide, slipping on the icy rocks.

"Is there really a pool for drowning women?" I ask him, panting.

He nods.

"Why did they have it?"

He says it was a killing method at that time. For punishment.

"What time?" I ask.

He looks confused.

"I mean what era was that? When did this happen?"

"Seventeenth century," he answers.

"What did they do to be punished this way?"

"Witchcraft, infidelity."

I run back to David and Allan, who are staring at one pool in particular. They've found a plaque bearing the names of all eighteen women who were drowned here. We gaze into the slow-moving water—not yet frozen over—looking for ghosts. I catch my reflection and jump back.

We return to Reykjavik for dinner at the Laundromat Café. I happily play cards with David and slurp down fish soup, even as beer and whiskey are poured for customers around me. Allan tries an Icelandic brew, and I admire its color but have no interest in its taste or effect. I order coffee, mostly for the warmth it offers.

We walk, ever so slowly, back to our apartment, enjoying the streetlights and falling snow. I notice lights coming from a shop below sidewalk level and bend down to look in the window.

A goldsmith is sitting at a chair with tools strewn across his desk. He's holding something in his hand. I put my face against the window to get a closer look. He's making a necklace with an anchor pendant.

I nod but he doesn't notice me.

Yes! I want to tell him. *You're making the right thing!* Three days in his island nation have delivered me to a realization that I never thought possible in all my years of swimming, drinking, and traveling.

I am anchored.

ACKNOWLEDGMENTS

Long after crossing the Empty Quarter with his Bedouin guides, British explorer Wilfred Thesiger said that the satisfaction in attaining a goal was in direct proportion to the hardship and challenge involved in getting there.

Going sober in Abu Dhabi was the greatest and most difficult adventure of my life and, thereby, the most rewarding. I emerged from the process with deep gratitude for the Middle East, a region that perplexes most Americans, for helping me find clarity.

I couldn't have done it without my husband, Allan Nicholls, who is always ready to go the distance with me. But I actually did it for my son as well as myself. I want David to grow up knowing there are ways to conquer our personal deserts and demons. I intend to be a beacon of hope and strength for him until the day my light goes out.

I must also thank my agent, Priya Doraswamy—brave and daring enough to push me into discomfort, just like my best swimming coaches, Dick Smith, Harry Carruth, and Bill Mann. I'm humbled that Erin Calligan Mooney, acquisitions editor with Grand Harbor Press, believed in my story within the first few pages of reading it and was willing to share it with the world. I have profound gratitude to Chad Sievers, who made my manuscript so much richer with his developmental edits.

Great appreciation also goes to my former colleagues in Abu Dhabi, whose names have been changed to protect their privacy. Thanks also to our dearest friends in Abu Dhabi, especially my dear sweet Simi Nourse in Al Ain, who read every page of this book at least twice, and helped me through my darkest days from near and far.

Last but not least, I extend my deepest gratitude to my extended family: Ashley and John Nicholls, Samantha and Andrew Nicholls, Barbara Rixey Darrow, Lee Bercaw, Nora Bercaw, Kathy Marshall Dion, Nancy Dunlap Bercaw, Pamela Scott Arnold, and Sandra Langley. Also many thanks to my soul sisters in Chicago; Portland, Oregon, and Portland, Maine; Mesa, Arizona; and up and down Vermont and the entire East Coast; as well as my Seoul sisters who are scattered around the world.

Of course, I can't forget my father, Dr. Beauregard Lee Bercaw, who's always with me in spirit—reminding me that I have the power to prevail anytime, anywhere.

ABOUT THE AUTHOR

Writer and national champion swimmer Nancy Stearns Bercaw is a seventeen-time NCAA All-American athlete and was inducted into the University of South Florida's Athletic Hall of Fame in 2009. Her writing has appeared in publications around the world, including the *New York Times*, the *Huffington Post*, the *Korea Herald*, *U.S. News & World Report*, Abu Dhabi's *Tempo* magazine, and MariaShriver.com. She is the author of *Brain in a Jar: A Daughter's Journey Through Her Father's Memory* and a contributor to *Chicken Soup for the Soul: Living with Alzheimer's and Other Dementias*. She lives in Vermont with her husband and son.